Alfred Edward Housman, 1910.

(Source: This image comes from the Google-hosted LIFE Photo Archive and is available on Wikimedia Commons. The photograph is in the public domain and I am not aware of any restrictions on its use.)

Contents

Preface

A study guide is an *aid* to the close reading of a text, *never* a substitute for reading the text itself. This guide helps readers to develop their own understanding and appreciation of Housman's poems; it does not provide ready-made interpretations to be accepted uncritically, absorbed and regurgitated.

Housman's poetry deserves to be read *reflectively*, and the aim of this guide is to facilitate such a reading. The Notes aim to clarify matters of fact and to suggest connections with other literary works. The Guiding Questions are designed to help the reader understand what each poem is about (its setting, characters, plot, themes, emotions, etc.) and how each poem is written (its verse structure, use of rhyme, imagery, symbolism, etc.). The meaning of a poem can only be fully appreciated when both *what* the poem says and *how* the poem says it are seen in combination. Another way of saying this is that the style of a poem makes an essential contribution to the reader's experience of the total meaning of the poem.

The questions do not normally have simple answers, nor is there always one answer. Consider a range of possible interpretations, preferably by discussing the questions with others. Disagreement is to be encouraged! However, if you are reading *A Shropshire Lad* on your own, you should consider keeping a reading journal in which you jot down your unfiltered reactions to each question, even if these are contradictory and confused. Such jottings will prove to be invaluable as a source when you decide that you are ready to firm up your response to each poem.

The Guiding Questions have *no* answers provided. This is a deliberate choice. The questions are for readers who want to come to *their own conclusions* about the text and not simply to be told what to think about it by someone else. Even 'suggested' answers would limit the *exploration of the text* by readers which is the primary aim of the guide. In my years of teaching literature, I found that students frequently came up with answers that I had not even considered, and, not infrequently, that they expressed their ideas better than I could have done.

The Final Thoughts on each poem attempt to draw the strands of the poem together into some sort of conclusion which represents my best understanding of each poem at this point in time. These commentaries do *not* set out to answer the questions, but often they *do* cover the same ground. For this reason, I would urge readers to answer the questions *before* reading the commentaries that I offer. The commentaries make no claim to be either comprehensive or definitive and should be read, and hopefully discussed, critically.

Acknowledgements

As always, I am indebted to the work of numerous reviewers and critics. Where I am conscious of having taken an idea or a phrase from a particular author, I have cited the source in the text and the bibliography. Any failure to do so is an omission that I will correct if it is drawn to my attention.

All of the poems reproduced in this book are free from copyright. In addition, I believe that all other quotations used in the analytical portions of my text fall under the definition of 'fair use.' If I am in error on any quotation, I will correct it.

Thanks are due to my wife, Barbara, for reading the manuscript, for offering valuable suggestions, and for putting the text into the correct formats for publication. Any errors which remain are my own.

Readers should bear in mind that while my own text is written in American English (since I live in the USA), Housman's poems and much of the literary criticism from which I quote are written in Standard English. The difference is most evident in variations in spelling.

A. E. Housman: A Timeline

1858-1876: The Worcestershire Years

1858 – June 17th: Edward Housman, a country solicitor originally from Lancaster, marries Sarah Williams in Woodchester, Gloucester.

1859 – March 26th: Alfred Edward Housman is born at Valley House in Fockbury, a hamlet on the outskirts of Bromsgrove, in Worcestershire, the county to the east of Shropshire. He will be the eldest of seven children. April 24th: Housman is baptized at Christ Church, in Catshill.

1860 – The Housman family moves to Perry Hall, Bromsgrove, where Housman spends his youth.

1870 – September: Housman enters King Edward VI School in Birmingham (later called Bromsgrove School) having won the first Cookes' scholarship there. His education emphasizes Greek and Latin studies. He reveals his academic promise and wins prizes for his poems.

1871 – March: Housman is sent to live with family friends because his beloved mother, Sarah, is seriously ill. On his twelfth birthday (March 26th), he receives a letter from his father telling him that his mother has died. Sarah's death from cancer at the age of forty-three has a profound effect upon him and may explain his life-long atheism. Years later he will write that he, "became a deist at thirteen and an atheist at twenty-one."

1872 – This is the year, Housman would later say, when he became a deist.

1873 – Edward Housman remarries. His choice is an elder cousin, Lucy, who quickly establishes a good relationship with all of his children.

1877-1882: The Oxford Years

In 1877, Housman wins an open scholarship of £100 a year to St John's College, Oxford, to study classics. 1878 – February 2nd to June 22nd: He is a co-founder, co-editor and contributor to an undergraduate magazine, *Ye Round Table: An Oxford and Cambridge Magazine*, featuring humorous verse and satire, at which he excels.

1879 – Housman gains a First in Classical Moderations ("mainly a matter of translation work" [Graves 46]).

1880-1881 – He takes rooms with his classmates A. W. Pollard and Moses John Jackson and apparently falls in love (for the first and only time in his life) with Jackson. There is no evidence that Housman actually reveals his feelings to Jackson but it is clear that Jackson, who is firmly heterosexual, does not have similar romantic or sexual feelings for Housman, though the two remain friends. Many of Housman's subsequent poems deal with unrequited love and presumably have their origin in the rejection he suffered when he was "one-and-twenty."

1880 – This is the year, Housman would later say, when he became an atheist.

1881 – He fails Greats which seems to end his prospects of an academic career. The reason for this failure has caused much speculation. Housman's biographer, Richard Graves, identifies five main factors: Housman's overconfidence having sailed through Mods.; his increasingly consuming interest in textual analysis, particularly the works of Propertius, who was not on the syllabus; his lack of interest in, or rather frank contempt for, Greek Philosophy, which was on the syllabus; the failure of his teachers to engage his interest; his father's declining health (only six days before his first examination Housman learned "that his father had suffered a stroke and was desperately ill" [Graves 54]); and his spending too much time with his friends, particularly his housemates Jackson and Pollard, instead of studying. He has to go back to Oxford for the Michaelmas term, returning home in December. He occasionally teaches the sixth-form at Bromsgrove School.

1882 – June: He sits the exam to gain a lowly B.A. degree and passes.

1882-1892: The Patent Office Years

1882 – July: Housman takes and passes the Civil Service examinations and in December moves to Bayswater to take a Higher Division clerkship in the Patent Office in London, largely because Moses Jackson already works there. Along with Moses's younger brother, Adalbert Jackson, the two share lodgings. Housman spends many of his evenings in the British Museum library studying Greek and Latin.

1885 – August: There seems to be a crisis in Housman's relationship with Moses that causes Housman to find new lodgings, though he and Jackson remain on friendly terms. In autumn 1887, Jackson goes to India to become Principle of Sind College in Karachi, India. Eighteen months later when Jackson returns to England to marry a young widow, Rosa Chambers, Housman is not invited to the wedding. The newly-weds settle in Karachi. Housman and Jackson will rarely meet again, but Housman will be godfather to one of Jackson's children and will lend Jackson a large sum of money when, many years later, Jackson retires to British Columbia and tries, unsuccessfully, to establish a farm there.

Housman pursues his classical studies independently. In 1885, Macmillan turns down his edition of Propertius being "not prepared to gamble on an unknown scholar" (Graves 68). A number of his scholarly articles on Horace, Propertius, Ovid, Aeschylus, Euripides and Sophocles are published in academic journals such as the *Classical Review* and the *Journal of Philology*, and they began to earn for Housman a high reputation for textual scholarship. The correction of scribal and editorial errors in classical texts (called 'redaction' i.e., determining the correct version of a classical text by comparing different manuscripts and judging which variant is the most likely), which he regards as an intellectual search for the truth, becomes his life's work and some would say his obsession. Housman

4

has no interest in the interpretation of the works of classical writers; he is solely involved in the investigation of manuscripts to establish reliable texts of their works.

During these years, Housman has also been producing original verse, though not for publication.

1892-1911: The University College London Years

1892 – April: Emboldened by the reception of his published work, Housman applies for, is elected to, and accepts the professorship of Latin at University College London. Housman will refer to himself as having been "rescued from the gutter."

It is during his nineteen years in this post (1892-1911) that most of his poems belong. Housman gains the reputation of being very withdrawn, unsocial, austere and unbending. Certainly, he is a perfectionist and does not suffer fools gladly. However, his close friends at this time respect, admire and like him; his students are awed and intimidated by his reserve, but they generally have the same opinion.

November: Adalbert Jackson, who, since the departure of Moses, has been Housman's closest friend, dies of typhoid. This trauma initiates an emotional explosion that results in Housman's composing many of the poems collected in *A Shropshire Lad,*

1894 – November: Death of Housman's father. Charles McGrath describes him as having been "a Dickensian figure – a jolly, heavy-drinking lawyer, often broke and given to investing in harebrained schemes" ("How A. E. Housman Invented Englishness," *The New Yorker*, June 19th, 2017).

1895/6 – Housman offers "Poems by Terence Hearsay" to the Macmillan Company, but it is rejected. Most of the poems in this collection are written in what he later describes rather vaguely as a period of "continuous excitement" in 1895. Housman's old friend A. W. Pollard suggests that the collection be retitled *A Shropshire Lad*. It is published in March 1886 in a first edition of five hundred (of which about one hundred and sixty are sent to the US) by the firm Kegan Paul at the author's own expense (a total of £30), but it sells slowly despite being well reviewed. At the end of two years, Housman's brother, Laurence, buys up the last few copies.

1897 – September 14th: Grant Richards, who will become one of Housman's life-long friends, publishes his first edition of five hundred copies of *A Shropshire Lad* which sells out. Housman declines royalty payments and encourages the production of cheap editions to keep the price down.

1898 – Housman's brother, Herbert, gives up his medical career and enlists in the Army as a private.

1900 – Grant Richards prints a further one thousand copies of *A Shropshire Lad*.

1901 – October 30th: Herbert Housman dies, aged 33, fighting in the Boer War in South Africa.

1902 – Grant Richards prints a further two thousand copies of *A Shropshire Lad*.

1905 – Housman's brother Robert dies, aged 45, after a short illness.

1906 – Sales of *A Shropshire Lad* suddenly take off. In the years 1906 to 1911, the book sells an average of 13,500 copies annually (Graves 119).

1907 – November: Housman's stepmother, Lucy, with whom he has always had a close relationship, dies aged 84 after a long illness.

1911-1936: The Trinity College, Cambridge, Years

Between 1903 and 1930, Housman publishes a five-volume critical edition of *Astronomicon* by the minor first century Latin poet Manilius, as well as editions of the works of Juvenal (1905) and Lucan (1926). Although Housman's early work and his responsibilities as a professor included both Latin and Greek, he begins to specialize in Latin poetry. When asked later why he stopped writing about Greek verse, he responds, "I found that I could not attain to excellence in both."

1911 – January: At the age of fifty-one, Housman becomes Kennedy Professor of Latin and a fellow of Trinity College, Cambridge, where he remains for the rest of his life.

Housman learns from his friend Moses Jackson that he has left India and moved with his family to British Columbia, Canada.

July 28th, 1914 to November 11th, 1918 – The Great War (or First World War). *A Shropshire Lad* finds a new generation of readers, particularly amongst serving soldiers and sales increase (1916, 14,500 copies; 1918, 16,000 copies) (Graves 174).

1922 – Housman receives news that his old friend Moses Jackson is gravely ill in Vancouver, Canada. This provides the impetus for Housman to revise existing poems and write new ones, so that his friend can read them. On October 19th, *Last Poems* is published by Grant Richards. The collection receives excellent reviews and the first printing of four thousand soon sells out. Richards orders a further seventeen thousand copies. A copy does reach Moses Jackson in time for him to read it before he dies of stomach cancer on January 19th, 1923.

1933 – Housman speaks publicly about his poems for the first time in the Leslie Stephen Lecture which he calls "The Name and Nature of Poetry." He argues that poetry is an emotional and physiological experience that should appeal to the emotions rather than to the intellect. Thus, it is the antithesis of his classical scholarship. The lecture is very well received though not amongst adherents of New Criticism.

1936 – April 30th: Housman dies, aged 77, in Cambridge after an extended period of increasing ill health due to heart disease. His ashes are buried at St Laurence's Church, Ludlow, Shropshire. A posthumous collection, *More Poems*, is edited and published by his brother Laurence.

Posthumous:

1937 – A. E. H.: Some Poems, Some Letters and a Personal Memoir by his Brother is published by Laurence Housman.
1939 – Housman's *Complete Poems* published.

My Favorite Housman Anecdote

Housman is in many ways an enigmatic figure: sometimes uncommunicative and antisocial to the point of rudeness, he could be both sociable and a brilliant conversationalist. Similarly, he was a man seen as the epitome of seriousness who delighted in playing practical jokes. The following story, perhaps apocryphal, is told by Basil Davenport in his Introduction to the Centennial Edition of Housman's *Collected Poems*:

> [A]t the close of one of his lectures, he announced, "My next lecture will be on the second satire of Juvenal. As this is one of the obscene satires, I request that the ladies absent themselves from this lecture." At the next lecture, a few daring women students did nevertheless appear; Housman surveyed them and said, "Since I see there are no ladies present, I will now lecture on the Second Satire of Juvenal." (1-2)

Davenport uses this story to illustrate his contention that Housman "hated women and resented their admission to the university" (1). He might, though he does not, have added that Housman could never remember his female students' names and had a tendency to reduce them to tears when he criticized their work.

Mr. Davenport (1905-1966), however, was an American academic (and a fine critic) who simply fails to understand Housman's dry sense of humor. So austere was his image that perhaps even some of those in the lecture hall could not bring themselves to acknowledge that Housman was joking – joking not, indeed, at the women who had bravely come to his lecture, but at the convention that held that the Second Satire of Juvenal was not appropriate for women. As for forgetting their names and making them cry, Housman was guilty of nothing more than treating his women students as students not as women.

Introduction to the Poetry of A. E. Housman

Let us be clear: A. E. Housman is a minor poet. For one thing, his output was relatively small. He published only two volumes of poetry during his relatively long life: *A Shropshire Lad*, 1896, and *Last Poems*, 1922; his Collected Poems contains one-hundred and seventy-five poems. Housman's poetry shows no discernible development either in thought or style; his range of themes is narrow (Virginia Woolf counted only, "May, death, lads, Shropshire"), gives his poems a repetitive quality; and technically his poetry is limited.

Some critics scarcely allow that Housman was a poet at all. Here are a number of critical opinions all tending to stress Housman's 'minor' status that I have arranged in descending order of vitriol:

> The truth is that many of Housman's poems are of a triteness of technique equaled only by the banality of the thought; others are slovenly, and a quantity are derivative… (Cyril Connolly, *New Statesman* article, 1936, reprinted in "A. E. Housman: A Controversy" in Ricks Ed. 36)

> [A] sustained reading [of Housman's poems] is best avoided. His concentrated and monotonous morbidity becomes enervating, no matter how skillful the variations. Housman, even at his best, should be taken in small doses, not only because of his monotony, but because of the emotional intensity of his monotonous theme. He soon exhausts even the most sympathetic reader. (Hamilton 25-26)

> Housman's major faults as a poet – the things that kept him a *minor* poet – are (a) the immature and commonplace nature of his subject-matter, all self-pity and grumbling; (b) the lack of development. Although he wrote poems over a period of some forty years, …[t]he last poems he wrote are no different from the first … Housman was not a very intelligent man; his poetry proves it. His poetry also proves that he was supremely, if narrowly, gifted. (John Wain, "Housman," in Ricks Ed. 27-28)

The critical backlash against Housman as poet began almost immediately after his death. No doubt much of it is unfair, and probably it was at least partly a reaction against the continuing popularity of his poems with the reading public – a cardinal sin to a certain type of literary critic. Nevertheless, these critics are not wrong. Housman can never stand as a poet alongside Chaucer, Milton, Keats, Wordsworth, or even his own favorite Matthew Arnold – and to suggest otherwise would be simply foolish.

The most apt and illustrative point of comparison, it seems to me, is with Housman's near-contemporary the American poet Robert Frost (1874-1963). Both were 'regional' poets (Shropshire and New England) who wrote about a traditional rural way of life that was already disappearing rapidly; both produced popular poetry written in traditional forms; both published their first collection relatively late in life (Housman was thirty-seven and Frost was forty); and so on. Yet there is no comparison between the range of the two writers, either in terms of their ideas or their mastery of form: Robert Frost was a great poet; A. E. Housman was a minor poet who wrote a few great poems.

Perhaps partly in reaction to the bitter attacks, a number of critics have sprung to the defense of Housman's poetry. Here are a number of critical opinions all tending to stress Housman's achievement in poetry that I have arranged in descending order of idolatry:

> The poems of A. E. Housman will endure as long as English poetry is read... (John Sparrow in Cyril Connolly, "A. E. Housman: A Controversy" in Ricks Ed. 47)

> At least twenty of Housman's poems are likely to live as long as the language. (A. W. Bateson, "The Poetry of Emphasis," in Ricks Ed. 131).

> It seems sometimes to a reader that Housman has only one poem to write, which he writes and rewrites tirelessly, though oftentimes with very brilliant and beautiful variations. (Cleanth Brooks, "Alfred Edward Housman," in Ricks Ed. 66)

> [T]he emotional range of his verse is limited, and unless there comes a time when beauty of expression is valued above all else in poetry, Housman will never be placed among the first rank of poets. But if ever there was a man who was truly inspired, it was Alfred Housman. Poetry welled up in him, poetry of mood and emotion, both powerfully heightened by the classical restraint of the verse-forms which he used. (Graves 240)

It seems that when it comes to Housman, the only position that is not viable is sitting on the fence: critics remain divided.

The Biographical Basis of *A Shropshire Lad*

> [Housman's] is a poetry, said Stephen Spender, which seems to hide some nagging Housmanish secret. One feels that the poem has its autobiographical aspect; and yet this is realized neither in the situation of the speaker of the poetic monologue nor in that of the "hearts that loved him." (Leggett *Theme and Structure* 3)

So much criticism on Housman's poetry in general, and on *A Shropshire Lad* in particular, has focused on its supposedly autobiographical nature that it is surprising to read in a letter to Maurice Pollet dated February 5th, 1933, Housman state that "very little in the book is biographical" and that his poetic outlook is "owing to my observation of the world, not to personal circumstances." As to the county of Shropshire itself, Housman simply states, "I was born in

Worcestershire, not Shropshire, where I have never spent much time."

So, A. E. Housman was not a Shropshire Lad, nor – at the time when he completed and assembled his first collection of poems – was he a lad at all. Nevertheless, the autobiographical critics have latched onto a statement he made twenty-six years after the publication of *A Shropshire Lad*, in a short preface to his second volume, *Last Poems*. Here he wrote that most of the poems in his first collection had been written "in the early months of 1895" and under a "continuous excitement." Unfortunately, this ambiguous phrase has become the starting point of a search for a personal crisis early in 1895 which may have acted as the genesis for the poems of *A Shropshire Lad*. There is certainly no shortage of suggestions, for Housman had suffered a number of disappointments and losses in the first twenty-five years of his life, but the hunt has proved to be ultimately frustrating and inconclusive. More than that, it is probably wrong-headed, for in a letter to Paul V. Love, an American, dated February14th, 1927, Housman stated, "The excitement was simply what is commonly called poetical inspiration" (quoted in Leggett *Theme and Structure* 9), and in his 1933 letter to Maurice Pollet, he made the following oft-quoted disclaimer:

> The Shropshire lad is an imaginary figure, with something of my temperament and view of life … I have never had any such thing as a 'crisis of pessimism'. In the first place, I am not a pessimist but a 'perjorist' [i.e., one who thinks the world is getting worse] … Secondly, I did not begin to write poetry in earnest until the really emotional part of my life was over; and my poetry, as far as I could make out, sprang chiefly from physical conditions, such as a relaxed sore throat during my most prolific period, the first five months of 1895. (Quoted in Marlow 150).

One of Housman's more endearing characteristics was his willingness to reply to readers of his work whom he did not know at all, but in this case, he was being less than totally honest. We can agree that very few of the incidents recorded in *A Shropshire Lad* were taken from Housman's own direct experience, but the "temperament and view of life" embodied in the poems certainly belong to Housman. The death of his beloved mother, his failure to graduate with Honors, the rejection of his offered love by Moses Jackson, and Jackson's later move to India were certainly crises that changed Housman's personality and world-view radically. Though not a single poem in *A Shropshire Lad* deals explicitly with any of these events, together they made him a poet – if only a minor one. Medically, the description "relaxed sore throat" makes no sense at all. What was relaxed during the period when Housman wrote most of his poems was his poetic voice, and there seems to be no reason to suppose that, like many authors, he did not write out of the wounds that life had inflicted on his psyche.

Housman was brought up in a conventional Victorian Christian family. His mother was a devout believer, and he never lost his respect for High Church Anglicanism as an institution, though her premature death robbed him of his faith in its tenets. Marlow writes:

> To call Housman a Christian, as some have done, is of course nonsense, but the bitterness at death and oblivion are more natural to one whose anger is because Christianity ought to be true and who can no longer believe in it ... (152)

Here, not in a particular incident or in a real or supposed sore throat, lies the fundamental biographical basis of all Housman's poetry.

The Process of Composition

By his own account, long afternoon walks, following lunch in a pub and a pint of beer, were the time when lines and whole stanzas of poems would spontaneously enter Housman's head unbidden, together with a vague idea of the poem's theme. Upon returning home, he would write these lines down in his poetry notebooks, leaving gaps where additional lines were evidently needed. Sometimes these would come to him spontaneously at a later date, and sometimes he would have to sit down and consciously work at them – normally, it was a bit of both. However, Housman was seldom content to leave lines of poetry in their original form. The notebooks show evidence of repeated re-writing and refining.

John Sparrow, perhaps Housman's most vociferous advocate, stresses that his poetry was both an emotional and an intellectual effusion. On the one hand, Sparrow writes that "Poetry was for him ... 'a morbid secretion', as the pearl is for the oyster. The desire, or the need, did not come upon him often, and it came usually when he was feeling ill or depressed..." On the other hand, Sparrow writes of the last poem in *A Shropshire Lad*, "Of its four stanzas, Housman tells us that two were 'given' him ready made; one was coaxed forth from his subconsciousness an hour or two later; the remaining one took months of conscious composition. No one can tell for certain which was which" ("A. E. Housman: A Controversy" in Ricks Ed. **47**).

The Arrangement of the Poems

A Shropshire Lad is a cycle of lyrical poems carefully selected from the body of work that Housman had already produced. At least seven poems excluded from this first collection would subsequently be included in his second collection, *Last Poems*, in addition to others that would not be published until after his death. Housman was adamant in his refusal to give permission for any of the poems in this first collection to appear in anthologies, though he had no such objection to the anthologizing of poems from his second collection. Similarly, he absolutely rejected every proposal to have *A Shropshire Lad* and *Last Poems* published in a single volume. All of this suggests strongly that Housman regarded the cycle of poems as a coherent whole.

Further, the poems selected were certainly not printed chronologically, and there is evidence in the printer's copy that Housman carefully revised the placement of several poems. We may reasonably conclude that he had some particular arrangement in mind or at least that the way the poems were arranged was of importance to him. Nevertheless, it would be a mistake to regard the collection as a carefully planned sequence and all attempts to do so have floundered on inconsistencies and contradictions (i.e., poems that do not fit where the proposed structure says they should fit and other poems that do not seem to fit anywhere). More pragmatically, Tom Haber points out that it is certainly possible to identify "blocks of poems here and there": the recruitment poems (I IV); poems of "a lover's sorrow after losing his heart" (XIII-XVI); "fatality overtaking one of two lovers competing for the desired one" (XXV-XXVII); and the homesick series (XXXVII-XXXIX); but he maintains that "this about sums up the serializing" (94). Haber goes on to identify individual poems that really do not fit in where they are placed and would not fit anywhere else in the cycle (XLII, XLIII and LXII) and comes to the conclusion that "rather than making thematic patterns of his poems ... Housman deliberately, for the most part, set his Shropshire Lad pieces against each other" (95).

In the broadest chronological terms, the sixty-three poems fall into four groups: the first is set in Shropshire (I-XXXVI); the second depicts journeys of different kinds, culminating in a description of the persona's departure from Shropshire to London (XXXII-XXXVII); the third is set in London (XXXVIII-LXI); and fourth (the final two poems) offers a retrospective commentary on the poems that have gone before (LXII-LXIII). Complementing this division, the poems in the first group are set in youth and springtime; they explore the theme of the awakening of innocence to the burdens of being human, specifically the persona's growing perception that death and decay are inevitable, and that love, like life's other joys, is fleeting. Those in the third group are set in adulthood and look back nostalgically on the lost golden world of rural youth; they examine the ways in which man endeavors to cope with the harsh realities of life. Thus, the cycle begins in a determination to live life to the full as an act of rebellion against human mortality, but it ends in stoical acceptance of ageing, decay and death. It is this that Leggett has in mind when he argues that "*A Shropshire Lad* does indeed contain a unity of theme and that it is structured to be read as a whole" (*Theme and Structure* 23).

Literary Influences

It is beyond the scope of this Guide to give more than a brief account of the literary influences that can be detected in Housman's poetry. Like many of his age and social class, Housman was raised on the King James Version of the *Bible* and knew it intimately. Haber calls it "by far the dominating literary influence in his poetry" (120), and Gordon Lea argues that "One of the most pronounced ironies [of *A Shropshire Lad*] involves Housman's antitheism, which is frequently vocalized in diction, phrases, and cadences either directly from, or highly reminiscent of, the King James Bible" (72). This can be seen not only in echoes of biblical language and the use of actual phrases, but more fundamentally in the mood and themes in Housman's poetry. He picks up on the sufferings inherent in life and on the inevitability of death, without, of course, accepting the Christian consolation of Divine Providence and Resurrection to Eternal Life.

The second most obvious influence is the British ballad. The traditional four-line ballad stanza rhyme (A B A B) occurs in over half of the poems in *A Shropshire Lad*, but it is in the dramatic, sometimes melodramatic stories of the ballads (crime and punishment, loving passionately, unrequited love, rivalry in love, murder, suicide and early death) that Housman's greatest debt lies. This is true despite the point made by Gordon Lea that "in actuality the cycle includes only three true ballads, 'Farewell to barn and stack and tree,' 'Is my team ploughing,' and 'the True Lover.' Of the remaining sixty poems in *A Shropshire Lad*, moreover, only fourteen conform to the quatrain pattern common to ballad verse (Numbers I, IX, XVI, XVIII, XX, XXII, XXV, XXXVI, XXXVIII, XXXIX, XL, LVII, LIX, and LX). And no one of this total of seventeen poems uses the conventional ballad rhyme scheme *abcb*" (73).

Housman himself recorded his debt to Shakespeare's songs which, as Tom Haber points out embody the same themes: "suicide for love, the ill conscience, innocence betrayed, the longing of age for the years of youth, the lament for the irrevocable dead" (136). Another influence Housman acknowledged was the German poet Christian Johann Heinrich Heine (1797-1856). Again, Haber points out the themes they have in common: "farewells to untrue love, fratricides, lovers returned from the grave, youthful criminals and suicides" (150). Being for decades the pre-eminent classical scholar of his age, Housman inevitably picked up much from classical poetry (particularly the Latin poet and philosopher Titus Lucretius Carus [c.99-c.55 BC]).

(For a more detailed and scholarly treatment of this topic, readers are referred to the books by Tom Haber and Norman Marlow. See Bibliography.)

Study Guide

Recurring Themes in Housman's Poetry

As of this writing (November/December, 2019), *A Shropshire Lad* has been continuously in print for just short of one hundred and twenty-five years. That fact may tell us nothing about the quality of Housman's poetry, but it does indicate that his poetry found, and continues to find, an audience. It does so because Housman writes about experiences to which his readers can relate. Davenport explains it thus:

> [Housman spoke] for all rejected lovers, for young men killed in battle, for those who are homesick for some land of no return, for those to whom the very beauty of earth is a reminder of its evanescence. Once or twice, too, he spoke for those who find it too hard to keep the laws of God and the laws of man, with just a hint of some personal tragedy. (1) … He speaks not only for rejected lovers and bereaved friends, not only for young men dead untimely, but to all who feel the tragic sense of life, to all who feel (even if the feeling is only a mood) that all human alternatives are unhappy. (8)

Hamilton provides the following data on the themes of *A Shropshire Lad*, "Of the sixty-three poems of *A Shropshire Lad*, thirteen are concerned with sexuality, six with war, ten with despair and disillusionment, and twenty-five with death in various forms – murder, suicide, capital punishment" (38). However, Cyril Connolly, ironically Housman's fiercest detractor, comes closer to capturing the essence of the popularity of these poems when he notes, "There are two themes in Housman: man's mortality, which intensifies for him the beauty of Nature, and man's rebellion against his lot" ("A. E. Housman: A Controversy" in Ricks Ed. 37).

It would be an error, however, to believe that the individual poems in *A Shropshire Lad* presents a consistent philosophy or even (to use a less academic term) view of the world. Leggett writes:

> The charge of inconsistency and contradiction is also leveled against Housman. Jacob Bronowski holds that the poems have no standard of value:
>> Every standard is called on, now in this poem, now in that.
>> Every poem is at odds with every other. For every poem
>> has a standard and makes a judgment of living: but
>> Housman has no standard.
> Hugh Holson states that Housman answers the philosophical questions he raises in contradictory ways, "The feeling that it is better to be alive than dead is vigorously expressed by a suitor [of one poem] …. Exactly the opposite opinion is expressed in another poem." (*Theme and Structure* 13)

Correctly, it seems to me, Leggett argues that such criticisms seeks to catch

Housman in a kind of 'Catch 22' [the coining of the term is mine not Leggett's], "In short, many commentators have pronounced Housman a philosophical poet only to reject his poetry because his philosophy is unsound or inconsequential" (*Ibid.* 12). Leggett also reminds us that in the Leslie Stephen Lecture for 1933 entitled "The Name and Nature of Poetry" Housman states unequivocally that poetry has to do with emotion not with thought saying, "'Meaning is of the intellect, poetry is not ... the intellect is not the fount of poetry ... it may actually hinder its production'" (*Ibid.* 16). It is important to bear these comments in mind as we review the themes of *A Shropshire Lad.*

'Shropshire'

Given the title and reputation of *A Shropshire Lad*, it comes as something of a surprise to learn that of the sixty-three poems in the collection, only fifteen directly reference Shropshire. Housman's county was Worcestershire and, by his own admission, he had hardly even set foot in Shropshire before publishing his first collection. He did, however, use *Murray's Handbook for Shropshire, Cheshire and Lancashire* as a work of reference and guide. In a letter dated February 5th, 1933, to Maurice Pollet, Housman admitted, "I know Ludlow and Wenlock, but my topographical details – Hughley, Abdon under Clee – are sometimes quite wrong."

Certainly, Housman did not place a premium on accuracy in his description of places in these poems. For example, "Hughley Steeple" describes the weather vane atop the steeple of the 13th / 14th century Church St John the Baptist as "bright, a far-known sign" and the graves of suicides as being located to the north of the church tower well away from those who had died respectable Christian deaths. Inspired by the poem to visit the church, Laurence Housman reported that the church was hidden in a valley and that the graves north of the tower were those of respectable church wardens and the wives of vicars. [We might add that St John the Baptist does not actually have a steeple but a squat, timber-framed belfry built about 1700 from which a very tall weather cock does rise.] In a letter to his brother dated October 5th, 1896, Housman accepted the accuracy of his brother's description:

> I ascertained by looking down from Wenlock Edge that Hughley Church could not have much of a steeple. But as I had already composed the poem and could not invent another name that sounded so nice ... I thought of putting a note to say that Hughley was only a name, but then I thought that would merely disturb the reader. I did not apprehend that the faithful would make pilgrimages to these holy places. (Quoted in Firchow *et al.* 8)

Laurence further claimed that his brother's description was based upon another place that had an ugly name so he simply substituted Hughley. We may agree with Firchow, however, that "Housman's Shropshire as a whole, and not merely Hughley, is 'only a name' to be found not on a map of England, but in A. E. Housman's mind alone" (*Ibid.*). Graves similarly concludes that "Shropshire is largely an imaginary land" (105).

All this being so, it seems reasonable to wonder why Housman made the choice that his protagonist and narrator, Terence, should be from Shropshire. Housman himself explained it this way, "'I had a sentimental feeling for Shropshire ... because its hills were our western horizon'" (quoted in Graves 105).

Two Fundamental Themes: The Loss of Innocence and Exile

There is a fundamental difference between the thought and mood of the poems which are set in Shropshire and those which are set in London. Leggett points out that, particularly in the first half of *A Shropshire Lad*, "A large number of the poems of *A Shropshire Lad* deal directly with the moment of insight and exhibit a progressive structure which carries the persona from innocence to knowledge or from expectation to disillusionment" (*Poetic Art* 63).

He identifies a second theme explored mainly in the second half of the collection in which Housman's persona:

> remembers how it was to have been young and ... captures in his memory of a blighted Eden the joy and pain of innocence as well as the gulf which now lies between him and his youth. In *A Shropshire Lad* this mood is signalled by the exile from the home shire and usually arises in the contrast between the Shropshire imagery, which recalls the state of innocence, and that implying the speaker's present exile (72).

Time and Mortality

The Church of England *Order for the Burial of the Dead* contains the following words;

> Man that is born of a woman hath but a short time to live, and is full of misery. He cometh up, and is cut down, like a flower; he fleeth as it were a shadow, and never continueth in one stay.
>
> In the midst of life we are in death: of whom may we seek for succour, but of thee, O Lord, who for our sins art justly displeased?
>
> Yet, O Lord God most holy, O Lord most mighty, O holy and most merciful Saviour, deliver us not into the bitter pains of eternal death.

Housman's poetry explores the human condition as described so graphically above, but without any hope of the Resurrection to Eternal Life promised by

Christian faith. Housman's art is founded on a pessimism that denies God: life is short and death inevitable. What is left is the tyranny of time, the relentless chronology that dictates the transience of life. Spring in Nature and youth in man are beautiful but pass quickly. Life offers neither lasting happiness nor justice, and ageing is such a painful prospect that an early death seems in many ways preferable.

The Shropshire poems are divided on the lesson to be drawn from this awareness of the brevity and inevitable decline that characterize life: sometimes, as in "Loveliest of Trees," it leads the protagonist to a more intense participation in life, but in other poems the result is not merely the acceptance of death but seeing death as a superior state. Thus, in "To an Athlete Dying Young," the youth is praised for leaving a world with his accomplishments intact. In contrast, the London poems are more accepting of life's harsh realities, but can recommend only stoical endurance. From the moment he is born, time is man's enemy, and even if he achieves his allotted three score and ten, human lifespan is an infinitesimal point compared with the eons of the universe. Edmund Wilson explains:

> [In his] poetry, we find only the realization of man's smallness on his turning globe among the other revolving planets and of his own basic wrongness to himself, his own inescapable anguish. No one, it seems, can do anything about this universe which 'ails from its prime foundation'; we can only, like Mithridates, render ourselves immune to its poisons by compelling ourselves to absorb them in small quantities in order that we may not succumb to the larger doses reserved for us by our fellow, or face the world with the hard mask of stoicism, 'manful like the man of stone.' ... [Housman's] world has no opening horizons; it is a prison that one can only endure. One can only come the same painful cropper over and over again and draw from it the same bitter moral. ("A. E. Housman," in Ricks Ed. 16)

The Cruel Universe

Housman regarded the universe as ultimately indifferent; it is not malevolent but, what is perhaps worse, meaningless. Man, confronted by the enormity of the universe, is the victim of blind forces over which he can have no control:

> From far, from eve and morning
> And yon twelve-winded sky,
> The stuff of life to knit me
> Blew hither: here am I. (XXXII)

Housman's biographer, Richard Graves, stresses that Housman's atheism developed much more gradually than Housman himself claimed. He describes the poet's beliefs thus: "[T]here is no God, and therefore there is no meaning or purpose in life; the Universe is indifferent, and man is no more than a speck of sentient matter doomed to a short and futile existence in a remote corner of the cosmos" (45). Graves adds:

> [I]f he believed that there was any guiding or controlling influence at work in the Universe, he believed that it was strictly impersonal. Lacking anything positive to live for, he badly needed to construct or adopt a solid philosophy which would give him some purpose for continuing to exist ... If there was no God, then to excel was at least to hurl back defiance at an unfriendly Universe, and to impose one's own order and meaning to it. (67)

The universe, created by chance or perhaps by a God who has abandoned it, is cruel and hostile. In the poem "Epitaph on an Army of Mercenaries" in *Last Poems*, professional soldiers must take up the slack for an uncaring deity: "What God abandoned, these defended, / And saved the sum of things for pay." However, in a world where "malt does more than Milton can / To justify God's ways to man" (LXII), poetry (and by extension art in general) can serve the purpose of inuring one to the harshness of reality; in a life that is fleeting, poetry can endure from generation to generation. Hamilton has this point in mind when he writes, "Housman did not deny all values: he believed in the aesthetic value of poetry; but he did deny any ultimate value" (1).

Rural v Urban Life

Housman was writing in the tradition of the pastoral which stretches right back to classical poetry. He accepts a foundational premise of pastoral poetry that a life passed close to the soil, surrounded by the natural world, is inherently superior to a life passed in the city. The poems set in Shropshire explore the paradox between the young persona's awareness of the beauties of nature and of social intercourse and his anguished recognition that these joys will soon pass. Exiled in London, the speaker reflects upon the absence both of natural beauty and the sense of being part of an organic community. All that appears to be left is the consolation of a stoical acceptance of human mortality. Thus, the speaker's progress from rural to urban life symbolizes the journey of life from youth to old age and death.

The natural world in Housman's poems is frequently lovely and offers man delight, but there is nothing in man's experience of Nature to offer him solace or to sustain him as, for example, the Romantic Poets and deists had found. Nature does not speak to man or offer evidence of a transcendent creator; instead, it brings on thoughts of death in Housman's poetry because plants and animals generally have even shorter spans of life even than does man. One difference, of course, is that flora and fauna lack consciousness of their mortality. Another is that the cycle of the seasons appears to be, if not eternal, measured in millions of years. In Nature, each spring marks a rebirth, while for man each spring brings him only closer to the grave.

Soldiers and Soldiering; Patriotism and War

Housman was not a war poet in the sense that the poets of The Great War (1914-1918) were: unlike them, he had no first-hand knowledge of military service. On the other hand, he did have a brother, Herbert, who joined the King's Royal Rifle Corp as a corporal, went to South Africa in 1899 to fight the Boers and made the ultimate sacrifice. Thus, Housman not only had an emotional connection with the subject of soldiering but, having read Herbert's letter home, knew something of the realities of the lives of serving men. Even without the personal interest which stemmed from his brother's enlistment, it would have been difficult for a politically aware (though not politically active) man like Housman to ignore the subject entirely. The second half of the nineteenth century was a period when the 'Empire on which the sun never sets' was a matter of national pride.

In the first poem of *A Shropshire Lad*, "1887," one of the few to be titled, the conventional patriotism of Queen Victoria's Jubilee is balanced by the irony that God can only save the Queen with the help of those who are willing to die for her sake: "The saviours come not home tonight: / Themselves they could not save." Housman frequently deals with the plight of the young soldier, and he is usually able to maintain sympathy both for those who are the victims of war and for the patriotic cause of the nation. Graves explains Housman's attitude to soldiers in general as a "complex mixture of emotions …: the homosexual interest, the admiration for courage and self-sacrifice, the compassion, tinged with envy, for those who died young and with honour…" (121).

Gay Love

The poems collected in *A Shropshire Lad* were carefully selected to exclude any that overtly referenced gay love (much more so than were those included in his other two collections, *Last Poems* and the posthumously published *More Poems*). The poems in his first collection offer Housman 'plausible denial' (a term used by politicians and government officials to describe the capacity plausibly to deny responsibility for or knowledge of wrongdoing because of a lack of evidence proving the allegation). Thus, when the poems speak of young men pining away because of unrequited love, they either reference a rather vaguely drawn heartless lass, or leave the reader to supply that detail by saying nothing of the gender of the beloved. To the contemporary reader, Housman's poetry is self-evidently about gay love, and no doubt it was to many of his, largely male, readers at the time – though this certainly never occurred to others who were somewhat more naïve on matters of sexual preference.

The facts are these: Housman had one great love in his life, Moses Jackson, who, being resolutely straight, did not return his feelings. The two greatest periods of Housman's productivity as a poet coincide with his rejection by Jackson and his anticipation of the final loss of Jackson to a long illness. That said, to the contemporary reader, the biographical inspiration of Housman's poems is entirely irrelevant. Being rejected by the person one loves is pretty much the same irrespective of the gender and sexual preferences of the two people involved.

One other trend in biographical criticism needs to be addressed. Various critics have sought to locate the source of Housman's pessimism about life and of his personal reticence in the internal psychological conflict caused by being a gay man in a time when that was not only illegal but also condemned as sinful and unnatural. I would not for a moment wish to minimize the pressures experienced (then even more than now) by gay people, nor am I qualified to make any definitive judgment on Housman's psychological state. However, I have come across no evidence whatsoever that Housman *did* suffer from any internal guilt over his sexual preferences or that he felt any guilt or remorse about acting upon them. There were other factors in Housman's life that impacted his psychic development and that are behind the content, mood and tone of his poems.

Pessimism or Stoicism?

Hamilton concedes that a few of Housman's poems may be "the finest short poems in our language," but insists "that his failures are the result of a false quality of emotion – pessimism degenerating into melodrama and sentimentality – rather than of craftsmanship or technique..." (61). Similarly, Robert Brown argues that "with the exception of five poems the entire volume sounds a note of pessimism." The poems that Brown singles out as exceptions are X, XV, XXII, LXII and LXIII, though he adds that four of these are "questionable," though unfortunately he does not elaborate on this comment (23). Brown concludes:

> It appears that the volume contains poems whose themes bear
> little cause for rejoicing and find the only hope in death ... a firm
> belief in the impossibility of love between man and woman ... a
> tragic vision viewed through the futility of the struggle of mortal
> existence ... it is in this pessimistic current that one finds the
> thread which holds the poems of the volume together, and, as a
> consequence, it is through this perspective of pessimism that the
> volume must be viewed as a unified work of art. (23-26)

We have seen that Housman himself rejected the idea that he was a pessimist and other critics have preferred to use the word stoicism to describe Housman's view of the world, stressing that he counsels a kind of dogged endurance as the proper response to the realities of human existence. Housman himself wrote in a letter to his sister Kate on the death in action of her son, Clement, "[T]he essential business of poetry … is to harmonise [*sic*] the sadness of the Universe, and it is somehow more sustaining and healing than prose" (quoted in Graves 140).

Stylistic Features of Housman's Poetry

Language

Housman made a conscious effort to capture human emotions through the use of plain, monosyllabic diction. The colloquial language of his poetry was both appropriate to the subject matter and made his verse accessible to a wide audience. Morton Zabel draws attention to Housman's "love of folk speech" as the essential to his best poetry:

> The aphoristic twang and irony of peasant idiom, grafted to the sophistication of the Horatian style, relaxed his temper, freed it from formulated stiffness and cliché, and gave Housman his true single medium as a poet – a verse style marked by a subtle irony of tragic suggestion, a tensile integrity of phrasing, a sense of haunting human appeals playing against the grim inexorability of law. ("The Whole of Housman," in Ricks Ed. 125)

A. W. Bateson offers the following data to illustrate the simplicity of Housman's diction:

> *A Shropshire Lad* has no five-syllable words at all. Apart from the hyphenated compound words, there are only seven four-syllable words in it, and with the same exception fifty-five three-syllable words. All the remaining words in the sixty-three poems are monosyllables and disyllables, and no less than twenty of the sixty-three poems have no words at all of more than two syllables. ("The Poetry of Emphasis," in Ricks Ed. 142)

Marlow writes of Housman that "He can get more out of a monosyllable that almost any English poet" (138).

The influence of the street ballads of the nineteenth century is seen in Housman's use of occasional archaic diction and syntax, in his constant reference to 'lads' and in the inclusion of references to everyday aspects of rural life from sports (e.g., running, football and cricket) to social activities (e.g., courting, going to the fair, and getting drunk). None of this came naturally to Housman who was not really a countryman of any shire, never worked on a farm in his life, did not play sports even as a young man, never courted a lady, would have avoided fairs like the plague, and (though a connoisseur of fine wines) never got falling-down drunk in his life. The simplicity of language is, then, like everything else in the poems a triumph of artifice.

Narrative

A strong narrative structure is apparent in most of Housman's poems. The narrator takes the reader through a series of recollected events and actions, which are often thought-provoking or provide an insight into the nature of life. His most common plot-line is the series of events that lead (or led) the narrator to a significant epiphany.

First-person Narrative Voice

It is generally accepted that, as reported by Housman's friend A. W. Pollard, the original plan was to publish his first collection of poems under the title *The Poems of Terence Hearsay*, the Shropshire lad whose voice would control the tone of the entire body of verse. Housman's name would not appear as the author of the collection.[1] The rustic persona Housman used bears little resemblance to himself except that Terence also has a highly developed sense of place and that he too forsakes the western county of his youth for the London of his adulthood. If he also appears to be obsessed by the same issues that we know to have troubled Housman (e.g., lost and unrequited love, human mortality, crime and punishment, etc.), his expression is that of a much younger man. John Stevenson notes that "In any of the roles, he is almost invariably characterized by his ingeniousness [i.e., innocence, naïveté, artlessness, simplicity] in the grip of a strong emotion, by what is often defined as on the threshold of discovery. He is awkward, but straightforward in his actions, and always in the process discovering results in a revelation of some kind'" (quoted in Leggett *Poetic Art* 46).

The lyrics in *A Shropshire Lad* draw on centuries of tradition in pastoral poetry. Leggett points to the crucial importance of this fact in understanding Housman's poems:

> William Empson has observed in *Some Versions of Pastoral* that the pastoral process works "by putting the complex into the simple." It is this process which we observe at work in *A Shropshire Lad.* The complexities of life have been reduced to a level which can be communicated, and this simplicity is made possible through the convention that the reader must accept in approaching the work – the poet is a rustic youth named Terence whose lack of sophistication and whose closeness to the primal forces of life allow him to comment meaningfully on the human condition. Only the naïve reader confuses the speaking voices of Housman and Terence. Housman, the sophisticated traveller, gourmet, and scholar, thus avoids the sentimentality which is always dangerously near in any comment on the great commonplaces of human experience such as life's mutability or the world's injustice. (*Theme and Structure* 151)

For this reason, it is always important to differentiate persona from poet. It is far too easy to assume that the voice we hear is that of the poet himself or that the poet automatically endorses what the narrator says. Remember that the first-person narrator is an imagined character in the poem in the way that a third person narrator is not. [The same is perhaps more obviously true of novels. *Lolita* [1955] is narrated by Humbert Humbert, a completely unreliable, self-delusional pedophile and murderer, a fictional character invented by the author Vladimir Nabokov.] With each poem we have to ask whether Housman intends his first-person narrator to be reliable or unreliable. Even if we conclude that the narrator of a particular poem is presented as totally reliable, we should still be cautious in simply identifying the narrator with the poet. At best, a first-person narrator can only be a simplified, fictionalized version of the complex human being who wrote the poem.

Graves helpfully explains the thinking behind Housman's choice of the name Terence Hearsay, "The Greek dramatist Terence was brought to Rome as a slave, and lived there in exile; no doubt Housman, thinking of his own exile in London from the world of his childhood, saw some similarity in their situations ... This use of 'Terence Hearsay' as a mouthpiece for his ideas helped to remove any inhibitions which had restrained Alfred's output of poems in the past" (101-102). As Leggett explains, "The pastoral mask, Terence, ... [became] a means of dealing with feelings and experiences beyond or below the range exhibited by the reserved bachelor" (*Poetic Art* 113).

Fortunately, the original title was abandoned and the collection was published as *A Shropshire Lad* under Housman's own name. As we read the poems, we realize that the first-person narrative voice cannot belong to a single individual, that it is sometimes ill-defined and sometimes hard to identify at all. There are also some dialogues between the speaker and others, including with those beyond the grave. The rustic observer and commentator on life is variously a lover, a criminal, a murderer, a soldier going off to war, a soldier in the heat of battle, a spirit, etc. Critics frequently comment adversely both on the adolescent nature of many of the ideas explored in the poems and the melodramatic and sentimental way in which they appear to be presented. This, commentators frequently argue, is why *A Shropshire Lad* has proved to be enduringly popular with adolescents (particularly males) and why it can never be satisfying to adult readers (presumably of either gender) who want something more complex, more nuanced. This would only be a valid criticism if Housman's was the voice in the poems, but it is not. What is often taken to be the poet's own adolescent verse is, Housman takes pains to make us understand, Terence's "stupid stuff" (LXII). He so brilliantly captures the mindset and idiom of the psychologically adolescent persona that critics mistake both for his own.

Housman's decision to publish under a pseudonym is often linked by critics to his sexuality and to his awareness of its very real legal dangers. In 1895, the year in which Housman was most productive in his writing, the publicity surrounding the persecution and imprisonment of the poet and dramatist Oscar Wilde, and the unconnected suicide of a young naval cadet at Woolwich because he identified in himself gay impulses that he thought sinful, meant that the issue had to have been at the forefront of Housman's mind. (He sent Wilde a copy of *A Shropshire Lad* while he was serving time in Reading Gaol [Jail].) However, Housman protected himself *not* by adopting the persona of Terence Hearsay, but by rigorously excluding all of those poems likely to be suspected of referencing gay love. Housman was happy to leave both his friends and readers to speculate upon the identity of the lady who might have excited such melancholy in the poet (a quest about as fruitless as trying to put a name to the Dark Lady of Shakespeare's Sonnets).

[1.] Pollard's claim to have suggested the title *A Shropshire Lad* from a phrase used in the collection has been questioned by Peter Firchow on the very reasonable basis that no such phrase occurs either in the collection itself or in Housman's notebooks. Firchow uses this as the opening salvo in his argument that Housman is not a true regional poem having neither a reliable ear for the voice of rural folk nor a reliable eye for the natural world of Shropshire.

Irony

Readers should not to take it for granted that Housman's poems unwaveringly endorse the beliefs (be those beliefs joyful, pessimistic, patriotic or sentimental) which they ostensibly assert. One distancing technique we have already analyzed is the use of a persona; another, equally important, is Housman's use of poetic form itself (rhythm, rhyme, diction, imagery, verse structure, etc.) to qualify or even criticize what in a prose paraphrase the poem seems to be saying. In fact, the defining characteristic of the poems that compose *A Shropshire Lad* is that they frequently undercut or seriously qualify what at first appears to be their message.

Verse Form and Rhyme

Writing most of his poetry before the first two decades of the twentieth century when formal practices were widely abandoned by 'Modernist' poets such as Pound and T. S. Eliot, Housman's poetry emphasizes the importance of traditional forms of rhyme and meter. He frequently uses the four-line ballad stanza, with an alternating rhyme scheme of A B A B.

Imagery

The imagery in Housman's poems is deceptively simple. As is evident from his lecture *The Name and Nature of Poetry*, he was deeply suspicious of the kind of imagery used by the Metaphysical Poets – what is called wit. To Housman, imagery that is too ingenious smacks of the intellect, and he strongly believed that poetry was not a product of the intellect.

Critical Reception

Throughout the 20th century, *A Shropshire Lad* proved to be more of a popular than a critical success. John Sparrow, perhaps the most vigorous defender of Housman's poetry, writes, "Because it expresses authentically the emotions, above all the unhappiness, of youth, and because its form is easy and its content has the charm of the simple, at times of the sentimental, his verse appeals almost unfailingly to those who themselves are young" (quoted in Ricks Ed. 5-6). The majority of critics, however, have on the one hand accepted the accuracy of Sparrow's observation and, on the other, seen in it the essential intellectual and stylistic limitations of Housman's work. To put it bluntly, they have held that if poetry is simple enough to appeal to ordinary readers, then it cannot be any good.

Looking back to his own youthful love of the collection, George Orwell [Eric Blair] analyzes in his essay "Inside the Whale" (1940) his own changing view of Housman's poetry:

> At the beginning of the period I am speaking of, the years during and immediately after the war [The Great War, 1914-1918], the writer who had the deepest hold upon the thinking young was almost certainly Housman. Among people who were adolescent in the years 1910-25, Housman had an influence which was enormous and is now not at all easy to understand. In 1920, when I was about seventeen, I probably knew the whole of the *Shropshire Lad* by heart. I wonder how much impression the *Shropshire Lad* makes at this moment on a boy of the same age and more or less the same cast of mind? No doubt he has heard of it and even glanced into it; it might strike him as cheaply clever – probably that would be about all. Yet these are the poems that I and my contemporaries used to recite to ourselves, over and over, in a kind of ecstasy

Orwell suggests that what made the poems so popular was the nostalgic appeal of their country setting to the increasingly urbanized middle class, "the picturesque side of farm life ... appealed to them — the ploughing, harvesting, stack-thrashing and so forth," and the attraction of reading about country rustics, "overcivilized people enjoy reading about rustics (key-phrase, 'close to the soil') because they imagine them to be more primitive and passionate than themselves." He adds that the poems' adolescent themes of murder, suicide, unhappy love, and early death which "deal with the simple, intelligible disasters that give you the feeling of being up against the 'bedrock facts of life,'" and that Housman's world view "was satisfyingly anti-Christian – he stood for a kind of bitter, defiant paganism, a conviction that life is short and the gods are against you, which exactly fitted the prevailing mood of the young [in the post-War decades]."

26

The themes of his poetry and his emotional handling of them mark Housman as an extension of the Romantic Movement that flourished in England in the early part of the 19th century and had a resurgence in the aesthetic movement of the 1890s. The critical evaluation of Housman's work in the two decades after his death in 1936 is tinged with the anti-Romanticism of that period. The directness and simplicity of much of Housman's poetry are viewed as faults. According to Richard Aldington, the influential critic I.A. Richards is rumored to have declared, "This had put us back ten years," after leaving Housman's Cambridge inaugural lecture, and Cyril Connolly, in a 1936 *New Statesman* article reprinted in Ricks's essay collection, says that Housman's poems "are of a triteness of technique equalled only by the banality of thought." He also talked about the limitations of the poet's themes of man's mortality and rebellion against his lot.

Housman's poetry, based as it is on emotion, never goes beyond what he can verify with his own feelings. This may have relegated him to a rank below that of the major poets of his age. "His world has no opening horizons; it is a prison that one can only endure. One can only come the same painful cropper over and over again and draw from it the same bitter moral" (Edmund Wilson). However, few writers have expressed this dark, if limited. vision with more poignancy and clarity than Housman.

A Shropshire Lad

1887

From Clee to heaven the beacon burns,
   The shires have seen it plain,
From north and south the sign returns
   And beacons burn again.

Look left, look right, the hills are bright,   5
   The dales are light between,
Because 'tis fifty years to-night
   That God has saved the Queen.

Now, when the flame they watch not towers
   About the soil they trod,   10
Lads, we'll remember friends of ours
   Who shared the work with God.

To skies that knit their heartstrings right,
   To fields that bred them brave,
The saviours come not home to-night:
   Themselves they could not save.

It dawns in Asia, tombstones show   15
   And Shropshire names are read;
And the Nile spills his overflow
   Beside the Severn's dead.

We pledge in peace by farm and town
   The Queen they served in war,   20
And fire the beacons up and down
   The land they perished for.

"God Save the Queen" we living sing,
   From height to height 'tis heard;
And with the rest your voices ring,   25
   Lads of the Fifty-third.

Oh, God will save her, fear you not:
   Be you the men you've been,

Get you the sons your fathers got,
And God will Save the Queen.   30

Notes

Read *"Dulce et Decorum est"* (1917) by Wilfred Owen, MC (18th March 1893 –
4th November 1918). It deals, though much more critically, with the same theme.
Read the St Crispin's Day speech that King Henry gives to rouse his troops before
the battle of Agincourt (*Henry V*, Act 4 Scene 3 Lines 18–67). Better still, go to
YouTube and watch several versions of it.

"1887" – Queen Victoria's Golden Jubilee, the fiftieth anniversary of her
accession, was celebrated on 20th June, 1887.

"Clee" – Clee Hill in Shropshire, England, near Ludlow (which was, in 1887, a
market town with just under 6,000 inhabitants) is part of a range of hills which
run over fifteen miles north to south. They are southeast of Wenlock Edge.

"God has saved the Queen" – The British National Anthem is "God Save the
Queen/King" (depending on the gender of the reigning monarch).

"tombstones show" – i.e., the light of dawn reveals the tombstones.

"the Nile" – The River Nile flows north through Egypt into the Mediterranean.
Until the middle of the twentieth century, the river flooded every year between
June and September as a result of melting snow and heavy summer rain in the
Ethiopian Mountains bringing fertility to the flood plain. The British Army had
fought The Anglo–Egyptian War (also called The British Conquest of Egypt) in
1882 against Egyptian and Sudanese forces led by Ahmad Oraaaby an Egyptian
nationalist.

"the Severn" – The longest river in Britain (220 miles) flows through the counties
of Shropshire, Worcestershire and Gloucestershire.

"the Fifty-third" – The 53rd (Shropshire) Regiment of Foot was a British Army
infantry regiment, raised in 1755. In 1881, it amalgamated with the 85th (King's
Light Infantry) Regiment of Foot to form the King's Shropshire Light Infantry.
The 53rd fought in Egypt and the Sudan.

"Get you the sons your fathers got" – Whether consciously or not, much of the
jingoism referenced in this poem recalls the battle speeches of King Henry in
Shakespeare's *Henry V* – particularly those before Harfleur and Agincourt. In the
former, he exhorts his men, "now attest / That those whom you call'd fathers did
beget you" (Act 3 Scene 1).

Guiding Questions

1. In the first three stanzas, the speaker makes a distinction between the people
who see the flame of the celebratory beacon "plain" and "bright" and those who
"watch [it] not." Who are the people in this second group? What promise does
the speaker make to them?

2. God has evidently "saved the Queen," since she has reigned for fifty years – but divine intervention has not been working unaided. Explain how the people in the second group have "shared the work with God."

3. The speaker calls those men who went out to defend the Empire "saviours." Comment on the possible irony in his use of this word. (Clue: Consider this from *Matthew* 27: 41-43: "Likewise also the chief priests mocking him, with the scribes and elders, said, He saved others; himself he cannot save. If he be the King of Israel, let him now come down from the cross, and we will believe him. He trusted in God; let him deliver him now, if he will have him: for he said, I am the Son of God.")

4. Comment on the speaker's use of antithesis (a rhetorical device in which two opposite ideas are put together in a sentence to achieve a contrasting effect) in lines 19-20.

5. How does the speaker emphasis the loyalty of the men who serve the Queen?

6. What implication about the future is contained in the final stanza?

Final Thoughts

A beacon burns atop Clee Hill seeming to stretch up to heaven in celebration of Queen Victoria's fifty years on the throne, just as it did to celebrate her coronation. God has evidently "saved the Queen." However, though many people see the celebratory beacon "plain" and "bright," those who have died sharing "the work with God" can "watch [it] not." These dead once "trod" the soil of Shropshire's hills and dales. The narrator speaks of them as lost "friends" and promises that they too will be remembered. At first, the speaker's attitude to God appears to be conventional, but in pointing out that God's work is "shared" by men (men who have laid down their lives in the cause), he introduces a subversive thought: the irony is that it was not God alone who "saved the Queen," it was the men from Shropshire who fought and died in her armies – they were "saviours" of the Queen, but paradoxically they could not save themselves.

There is a contrast between the exotic east, "Asia" and "Nile," and the homely "Shropshire" and "Severn," and between "tombstones" which carry connotations of death and "farm and town" with their connotations of life and fruitfulness. Similarly, there is a tragic irony in the "dawn" revealing the names of the dead on "tombstones," for these men do not see the dawn – they are denied the rebirth that the sun brings to the earth.

In the same vein, the speaker plays on the antithesis between the living who "pledge in peace" and those who "perished" "in war." The tone of this word-play is bitter; there is real anger (or at least sorrow) behind the apparently conventional sentiments expressed in traditional rhyme. Each quatrain rhymes A B A B. The rhyming words are almost all monosyllables and full rhymes. The odd lines are written in iambic tetrameter (four iambs per line, e.g., "From **Clee** to **heaven** the **bea**con **burns**") and the even lines in iambic trimester (three iambs per line, e.g.,

"The **shires** have **seen** it **plain**").

It is not the speaker's purpose to criticize now discredited notions of Empire and Colonialism, but to honor the patriotism and the bravery of the lads of Shropshire who have preserved their country at the cost of their lives. The speaker's bitterness, however, comes to the surface in his exclamation, "Oh, God will save her, fear you not." Our thoughts, he implies, should be for the safety of those who fight for Queen and Country, and particularly for those who will find their graves in some foreign field. And, he tells us, it will go on for generations: if the ordinary men of Shropshire "Get ... the sons [their] fathers got," then they too will give their lives that men may say God saved the Queen. Evidently the message of the poem is more ambiguous than it at first appeared to be.

Cleanth Brooks argues that a poem which the reader initially assumes will be a conventional celebration of the accomplishments of the Queen soon turns into a satire on the "sanctimonious hypocrisy of saying that God and Queen are responsible for the Empire when actually the Empire has been won at the cost of countless Shropshire lives –" ("Housman's '1887'" *Explicator* Volume 3 1944). Similarly, Robert Brown believes that the poem "expresses an ironic and sardonic note on the hypocrisy of an undeserved loyalty to the Queen" (8), and following the same line of interpretation the author Frank Harris once complimented Housman on the "bitter satire" of the final stanza and the way he had "poked fun at the whole thing [i.e., patriotism] and made splendid mockery of it." Such a reading of "1887" seeks to turn A. E. Housman into the Wilfred Owen (1893-1918) of *Dulce et Decorum Est* (1917-1918) who denounces those who:

> ... tell with such high zest
> To children ardent for some desperate glory,
> The old Lie: *Dulce et decorum est*
> *Pro patria mori.*

To do so flies in the face of Housman's own response to Harris, "I never intended to poke fun, as you call it, at patriotism, and I can find nothing in the sentiment to make a mockery of: I mean it sincerely; if Englishmen breed as good men as their fathers, then God will save their Queen" (quoted by Cleanth Brooks, "Alfred Edward Housman," in Ricks Ed. 76). As Brooks points out, however, this does not mean that the poem is not characterized by "a mature and responsible irony whose focus is never blurred" (*Ibid.* 78), by which he means that the poem is not cynical about genuine patriotism but remains *realistic* about what it means to the sons of Englishmen – and Englishwomen.

Central to the meaning of the poem, then, is the ironic contrast between its ostensible celebration of the permanence and stability of the British Empire and the speaker's evident awareness of historical time and place: something of permanent value (the Empire) depends upon the premature passing of men whose lives are inherently short and impermanent. Two dates establish the start and end of the period under consideration: 1837 and 1887. Within this slice of chronological time, the Queen remains unchanged, but the lads who joined the ranks of her armed forces are (to use the words of W. B. Yeats in "Easter, 1916") "All changed, changed utterly," for they have exchanged their vibrant youthful life for and the eternity of death. In this way, the speaker interjects his own awareness of human mutability

II

Loveliest of trees, the cherry now
Is hung with bloom along the bough,
And stands about the woodland ride
Wearing white for Eastertide.

Now, of my threescore years and ten,   5
Twenty will not come again,
And take from seventy springs a score,
It only leaves me fifty more.

And since to look at things in bloom
Fifty springs are little room,   10
About the woodlands I will go
To see the cherry hung with snow.

Notes:

You might want to find definitions of 'mindfulness' and 'peak experience.'
Read "Ode to Melancholy" (1819) by John Keats (1795-1821). It also deals with
human mortality.
I strongly recommend looking on YouTube for the clip from *Dead Poet's Society*
where Mr. Keating (played by Robin Williams) tells his students to "seize the
day" ("*carpe diem*") – to live their lives to their full potential because each of
them will eventually die. The Roman poet Horace (65-8 BC) wrote, "*Carpe diem,
quam minimum credula postero,*" which means, "Seize the present rather than
placing your trust in the future."
"the cherry" – In the U.K., cherry trees are in blossom from mid-April to early
May. The speaker uses the singular noun, but he is not talking about a single
cherry tree but about the whole species. And he is not really just talking about
cherry trees either: the cherry may be the "loveliest" of trees, but it stands as a
symbol for all the beauties of Nature which show in the newest forms in spring.
That is why later in the poem he determines to look out for the beauty of all
"things in bloom."
"hung with bloom" – Compare *Acts of the Apostles* 5:30, "The God of our fathers
raised up Jesus whom you murdered by hanging on a tree."
"ride" – This simply means 'path' – perhaps a path worn by people riding their
horses (i.e., a bridle path). I do not think that we have to assume that the speaker
is riding or in a carriage – he could be walking.
"threescore years and ten" – A score is twenty. This phrase is commonly used to
describe the span of human life, most notably in *Psalms* 90: "The days of our
years are threescore years and ten; and if by reason of strength they be fourscore

years, yet is their strength labor and sorrow; for it is soon cut off, and we fly away."

Guiding Questions:

1. Comment on the speaker's use of the superlative "Loveliest" and the verb "hung." What do these together add to the reader's impression of the cherry blossom?
2. In line one, what does the use of the word "now" and of the present tense imply about the blossoming of the cherry trees?
3. Is the speaker being entirely serious when he says that he "only" has "fifty more [years] to live and in calling that span of time a "little room"?
4. What idea does the speaker come up with as a way to extend the time he has to appreciate the beauty of the cherry blossom?
5. Comment on the poem's closing metaphor. (The cherry trees are *not* "hung with snow" they are "hung with bloom.")

Final Thoughts:

The second lyric continues the theme of mutability explored in the first. The voice in the poem is that of a young man of twenty. As befits a poem in the pastoral tradition, the speaker appears to be a perfectly ordinary countryman, either out for a ride or a walk in the countryside. He is no academic philosopher, yet in his own untutored way he communicates thoughts which go to the core of life's complexities.

The first word of the poem is a superlative: the cherry is the "Loveliest" of trees, in its most beautiful state – blossom-time. Notice also the strength of the first verb: the tree is "*hung* with bloom along the bough" suggesting the sheer weight of flowers. (Compare "To bend with apples the moss'd cottage-trees" from "To Autumn" by John Keats.) The word "hung" also implies a hand (God's?) decorating the tree with blossom (as one decorates a Christmas tree), but this is an idea that is not pursued and may even be rejected later in the poem. The word "hung" has, of course, a much more negative association with death. This idea *is* pursued in the poem.

In moments of peak experience (the term was first used by American psychologist Abraham Maslow) we feel the sheer joy in being alive. Such feelings appear to happen when we *notice* something and really *focus* upon it – or rather, we focus on the state of being conscious or aware of something. The cherry blossom is perfect "now," but "now" will not last: the transient splendor of the cherry blossom is what makes the speaker aware of his own mortality. The blossom wears "white for Eastertide," a personification which has connotations of spring brides; white is also the prescribed color of altar cloths during Easter. The white of the trees symbolizes purity, fresh beginnings, rebirth and innocence.

34

White is often associated with Christ, which seems to be referenced in the mention of Easter. However, the reader will recall that shortly after Christ entered Jerusalem he was arrested and crucified. For Christians, of course, this was merely a prologue to the resurrection, but then Housman was no Christian, and the cherry blossom will not be resurrected. "In my beginning is my end," writes T. S. Eliot in "East Coker," the second of his *Four Quartets*.

The second stanza seems dominated by numbers. The speaker is in the springtime of his life, just as the natural world is in its spring. There is surely something a little comic in the speaker's feverish calculation of how much time he has left. We see this in the contrast between the adverb "only" and the idea of "fifty [years]," and in the exaggeration of calling half a century a "little room." We call this sort of sudden insight an epiphany (i.e., a moment when a person, real or fictional, is suddenly struck with a life-changing realization). What the speaker comes to understand about his mortality is hardly original, but it is fair to say that it is not one that usually occurs to young people. Peter Firchow argues that this poem is a "failure" and locates the reason partly in "the characteristic abstraction ... of the natural elements," but even more in:

> The heavy-handed manner in which the turning movement is carried out in stanza two. It is simply too convoluted and verbose; it attempts too obviously to delay, by means of elementary arithmetic, the final superimposition of the two cherry trees, and therefore to produce a more intense 'shock'. It is not surprising, therefore, to discover from the evidence of the manuscript of the poem that Housman wrote the first and last stanzas before he wrote the second, which 'was evolved with some difficulty.'" (Firchow *et al.* 18-19)

Perhaps ... or perhaps there is an undercutting irony in all this calculation that Firchow misses.

In the final stanza, the speaker comes up with a partial solution to the dilemma of the fleeting nature of cherry blossom time: he will observe the cherry trees in winter when they will be covered snow, a sight in which he can find equal joy. Spring does not have the monopoly on beauty and this clearly also applies to his own life. He is now (at age twenty) in the springtime of life, but moments of peak experience will be possible right to the end of his life.

The speaker is in danger of falling victim to melancholy. In "Ode to Melancholy," John Keats writes:

> She dwells with Beauty—Beauty that must die;
> And Joy, whose hand is ever at his lips
> Bidding adieu; and aching Pleasure nigh,
> Turning to poison while the bee-mouth sips:

Life is indeed, short, and beautiful moments are transitory: the short poem itself begins in spring (season of regeneration) and ends in winter (the season of death).

One can either give in to despair or continue to be excited by the beauties of life. This is not, however, a Romantic poem: there is no relationship between Nature and man. Nature is indifferent. Man does not find God through the experience of Nature (the deist perspective), not does Nature wait on man to enjoy its loveliness, but that loveliness nevertheless exists.

The final line is, however, deliberately ambiguous, "I will go / To see the cherry hung with snow." Even in the midst of blossoming spring's rebirth and renewal, the speaker cannot shake his awareness of the inevitability of death – spring blossom *is* winter snow because, "In my beginning is my end" (the personal moto of Mary Queen of Scots). Far from being depressed by that reality, however, it inspires the speaker to enjoy his life in the full knowledge that it will end in fifty years. In regard to the loveliness of the cherry "wearing white," he determines not only to appreciate to the full the beauty of cherry blossom each spring (after all, he is already doing that), but to double his opportunities for observing such loveliness by showing the same appreciation of the cherry tree in winter when it is snow-covered. By extension, the speaker is also saying that just as spring holds no monopoly on beauty, so youth holds no monopoly on the experience of beauty.

The basic meter of the poem is iambic tetrameter, that is, each line has four iambic (unstressed / stressed) feet (e.g., "Is **hung** / with **bloom** / a/**long** / the **bough**" and "It **on**/ly **leaves** / me **fif**/ty / **more**."). However, Housman is flexible in his use of meter. The very first line, for example has nine syllables ("**Love**/li/est / of **trees**, / the **cher**/ry **now**"). You might scan the line differently as to stressed and unstressed syllables, but there certainly are nine syllables. In contrast, line four has only seven syllables ("**Wear**ing / **white** for / **Ea**ster/tide."). As a result, the first three feet are not iambs but trochees (i.e., a stressed syllable followed by an unstressed syllable), so such lines are trochaic tetrameter. The one thing that the lines have in common is that their rhythm brings out the alliteration ("bloom … bough" and "Wearing white"). The Shmoop editors add this comment:

> This rhythmic shake-up is there for another reason, too. "Loveliest of Trees" is a poem about change. The speaker keeps reminding us that it is the spring time, but that the spring won't last forever (hence the branches "hung with snow"). The shifting meter of the poem, then, mirrors the poem's themes of seasonal change (both in life, and in nature). (Shmoop Editorial Team. "Loveliest of Trees Form and Meter." *Shmoop*. Shmoop University, Inc., 11 Nov. 2008. Web. 13 Sep. 2019.)

The poem is comprised of three quatrains (i.e., stanzas of four-lines), each of which in turn is comprised of two rhyming couplets (A A B B). Unlike the meter, there is no variation. This prompts the Shmoop editors to add:

> The regularity of the rhyme scheme balances the see-saw effect of the meter, and suggests that seasonal change (winter-spring-

summer-fall, youth-old age-death) is a fact of life, one that is as
regular as clockwork. (*Ibid.*)
Whether rhyme and rhythm can be so closely connected to the meaning of a
poem is a matter of opinion.

III   ***THE RECRUIT***

Leave your home behind, lad,
  And reach your friends your hand,
And go, and luck go with you
  While Ludlow tower shall stand.

Oh, come you home of Sunday   5
  When Ludlow streets are still
And Ludlow bells are calling
  To farm and lane and mill,

Or come you home of Monday
  When Ludlow market hums   10
And Ludlow chimes are playing
  "The conquering hero comes,"

Come you home a hero,
  Or come not home at all,
The lads you leave will mind you   15
  Till Ludlow tower shall fall.

And you will list the bugle
  That blows in lands of morn,
And make the foes of England
  Be sorry you were born.   20

And you till trump of doomsday
  On lands of morn may lie,
And make the hearts of comrades
  Be heavy where you die.

Leave your home behind you,   25
  Your friends by field and town
Oh, town and field will mind you
  Till Ludlow tower is down.

Notes:

You might like to read "The Soldier" (1914) by Rupert Brooke (1887-1915). It has a similar theme.

Search the Web for 'World War I recruiting posters' to see how men were made to feel unmanly and cowardly for staying at home while their friends were going off to fight. Housman's poem, which predates the Great War, exploits some of the same language.

"Ludlow tower" – Ludlow is a market town in Shropshire. The parish church, St Laurence's, the largest in the county, has a particularly tall tower. "The tower is 135 feet (41 metres) high and commands expansive views of the town and surrounding countryside" (Wikipedia contributors. "St Laurence's Church, Ludlow." *Wikipedia, The Free Encyclopedia*. Wikipedia, The Free Encyclopedia, 20 Apr. 2019. Web. 14 Sep. 2019.).

"of" – i.e., on.

"The conquering hero comes" – "See, the Conqu'ring Hero Comes!" is a song from Part Three of George Frideric Handel's *Judas Maccabaeus* an oratorio composed in 1746. It was translated into many languages. The tune also gained familiarity as it was commonly played by brass bands at the opening of new railway lines and stations in Britain during the 19th century.

"will mind you" – i.e., will keep you in mind, remember you.

"lands of morn" – Lands far east of England (i.e., lands, like India, where dawn comes earlier than it does in England). In various European cultures, the East is called 'the Land of the Morning.' It might also mean 'newly discovered/colonized lands, countries new to civilization.'

Guiding Questions:

1. In the first stanza, what attitude does the speaker take to those young men who enlist in the army and leave not only their home towns but their home country to serve abroad?

2. Stanzas two and three quickly transition to thoughts of these same young men returning after their military service. How do these lines establish a sense of the community of Ludlow town?

3. Lines 13 and 14 have a very different tone from those that have gone before. What is the nature of the change? What new idea is introduced in these lines?

4. Stanzas five and six similarly each has a very different tone. Explain the contrast between the two.

5. What promise does the speaker make to the young men who serve (and more particularly to those who are killed serving) abroad? Does the poem present this as an adequate form of compensation for the sacrifice these men have made?

Final Thoughts:

The voice of the first stanza sounds very like that of a recruiting sergeant urging a young man to 'Serve Queen and Country.' It begins, as do stanzas four and seven, with an imperative verb. In stanzas two and three, the same speaker, having skipped entirely the period of the young man's service abroad, paints a joyful picture of his return as a hero. Ludlow is described as a vibrant community with people flocking either to church on Sunday or to the Monday market, and the returning hero appears to have no difficulty in fitting right back in. [In reality, as we in the USA know only too well, veterans frequently find it very difficult, even impossible, to reintegrate into civilian life.] The soldier is welcomed back having returned "victorious" from the wars.

Stanza four changes tone. Just as Spartan women were supposed to have told their husbands and sons to come back with their shields or on their shields (another way of saying, 'Victory or death'), so now the speaker establishes a high level of expectation, "Come you home a hero, / Or come not home at all." This too is patriotic jingoism, but once the idea of death is introduced it seems to overshadow the jingoism. Stanzas five and six offer contrasting pictures of the fate of the recruit: he will rise every morning to the bugle call, "And make the foes of England / Be sorry you were born," or he will lie in his grave until the bugle call that signals doomsday, "And make the hearts of comrades / Be heavy where you die." Notice the precise parallel between these two statements: the grammatical structure is identical and only key words differ. The stark choice that the recruit will face is to make the enemy suffer or to make their comrades suffer. This is emotional blackmail – the author, though not apparently the speaker, is fully aware of that.

The fourth lines of the first, fourth and seventh stanzas are also carefully paralleled with those lines in the first stanza. Again, the meaning is carried by the words that change in the final stanza. The high and ancient tower of Ludlow church is introduced as a timeless symbol of endurance and permanence applied to the loyalty of the recruit's friends and acquaintances, but note the progression. The speaker begins by saying, "While Ludlow tower shall stand" which is a positive statement, suggesting an indefinite span of time. By the middle of the poem this has become, "Till Ludlow tower shall fall" which is much less positive since it acknowledges that the tower *will* fall, though that time may be long into the future. Finally, the speaker says, "Till Ludlow tower is down" which is a negative statement because it includes finality. Note how the future tense "shall" has been replaced by the continuous present tense "is," and the strong rhyme on "down." Ludlow tower has stood for five hundred years, but it *will* fall – and the soldiers who go off to die in war will be long remembered but, ultimately, they will be forgotten. The speaker's ostensible message is thus undercut by the way in which Houseman develops the image of Ludlow tower to suggest that memory, like the tower, will in reality be subject to decay. In this way, the poem subverts its apparently patriotic message, or as Leggett puts it, "the sentiments of the persona are denied by the poem itself" (*Poetic Art* 52).

Robert Brown is surely wrong in arguing that this poem "is a piece of satire through a view of traditional hypocrisy just like '1887'" (8). His interpretation of the first and third poems in the sequence leads him to find in them no "thematic alliance" with the second poem which "is concerned with contrasting the beauty of nature with the brevity of life" (*Ibid.*). The mistake here is to see Housman's target in "1887" and "The Recruit" as being British Imperialism – a theme certainly absent in poem II. All three poems are united, however, by the theme of human mortality. Each poem describes the human tendency to strive for permanence (an Empire on which the sun never sets, the joy of natural beauty, the memory of dead friends), but in each case the aspiration for permanence is futile given the transience of human life. All things shall pass despite our best efforts to make them stand unchanging and still.

Each stanza rhymes A B C B, which gives the final line more power since it completes the pattern. The basic meter is iambic trimester (each line has six syllables that alternate stressed and unstressed accents), but several lines have an extra syllable and some lines (particularly those that begin with an imperative verb) open with a stressed syllable. The one constant is that the third line in each stanza always has seven syllables and the final line always six and always in three regular iambic feet. Thus, each stanza ends with a strong final line.

IV   ***REVEILLE***

Wake: the silver dusk returning
  Up the beach of darkness brims,
And the ship of sunrise burning
  Strands upon the eastern rims.

Wake: the vaulted shadow shatters,   5
  Trampled to the floor it spanned,
And the tent of night in tatters
  Straws the sky-pavilioned land.

Up, lad, up, 'tis late for lying:
  Hear the drums of morning play;   10
Hark, the empty highways crying
  "Who'll beyond the hills away?"

Towns and countries woo together,
  Forelands beacon, belfries call;
Never lad that trod on leather   15
  Lived to feast his heart with all.

Up, lad: thews that lie and cumber
  Sunlit pallets never thrive;
Morns abed and daylight slumber
  Were not meant for man alive.   20

Clay lies still, but blood's a rover;
  Breath's a ware that will not keep
Up, lad: when the journey's over
  There'll be time enough to sleep.

Notes:

Read "To the Virgins, to Make Much of Time" (1648) by Robert Herrick (1591-1674). It has a similar theme.
Go to YouTube and search the song "Get Up Jimmy Newman" by Tom Paxton, the American folk singer.
"Reveille" – A sunrise bugle or drum call to wake up everyone on a military post. The French verb translates as 'wake up.'
"dusk" – Dusk is generally the darker stage of twilight, the stage of evening just before darkness falls. In this case, it is when the darkness of night begins to give

way to the morning light.

"Strands" – i.e., strands itself, runs aground.

"the vaulted shadow" – i.e., darkness like a stone dome.

"Straws" – i.e., to lay straw around plants to protect them from frost – synonym: strews.

"'Who'll beyond the hills away?'" – Perhaps a conscious reference to the traditional British song, "Over the Hills and Far Away" which dates back to the 17th century. It exists in many versions. That from George Farquhar's play *The Recruiting Officer* (1706) contains the lines: "Over the Hills and O'er the Main, / To Flanders, Portugal and Spain, / The queen commands and we'll obey / Over the Hills and far away."

"belfries" – Not, in this case, church bells, but the alarm-bells of a watch-tower (remember the recruit is in hostile territory).

"trod on leather" – i.e., wore shoes, walked.

"thews" – i.e., muscles and tendons.

"cumber" – i.e., encumber, clutter up or burden.

"pallets" – i.e., crude, makeshift army beds.

"Clay" – Man was formed by God out of the inanimate clay, "And the LORD God formed man of the dust of the ground, and breathed into his nostrils the breath of life; and man became a living soul" (*Genesis* 2:7 King James Version). Similarly, man will return to clay at death, "In the sweat of thy face shalt thou eat bread, till thou return unto the ground; for out of it wast thou taken: for dust thou art, and unto dust shalt thou return" (*Genesis* 3:19 King James Version).

"blood's a rover" – i.e., roving is in the blood – it is in man's nature.

"a ware" – i.e., a commodity. ('Breath' is a synecdoche for life. Synecdoche is a figure of speech in which a part of something is made to represent the whole.)

Guiding Question:

1. The first two stanzas describe the stages of dawn from the first glimmerings of light until the moment when the sun rises high enough to illuminate everything. Examine the metaphors that the speaker uses in this evocative description. (Clue: I found six.)

2. What does the opening of each of the first three stanzas have in common?

3. Stanzas three to six each contains a different argument to convince the sleeper to get out of bed and start experiencing life. Explain each argument.

4. The poem is rich in alliteration. What does this add to your experience as a reader? (Clue: Read it aloud.)

Final Thoughts

Lisa Spurgin sums up "Reveille" better than I can:

[T]his poem is not a harsh blow akin to being doused in cold water; its ability to wake comes in its atmospheric description, its sounds, its sights, its internal vigour and liveliness. It's not just about physically waking, clambering from the covers and pulling yourself upright but waking yourself mentally, awakening to the world around you with all its possibilities. (The Reader, "Featured Poem: Reveille by A. E Housman." *blog.thereader. org.uk.* 18 Apr. 2011. Web. 13 Sep. 2019.)

The poem depicts the journey of life from youth (dawn) to old age (darkness). It begins with an evocative description of dawn. The moments before sunrise are like "dusk returning," moving, like the tide, "Up the beach of darkness." The dusk is "silver," a precious metal, which is the first indication of the value that the speaker places on time. Notice the strength of the verb "brims" which is augmented by the hard 'b' alliteration. Sunrise is a blazing ship lighting the eastern horizon. The "vaulted shadow" (an architectural metaphor) of night has been shattered and trampled (note the strength of the verbs the speaker uses) Darkness, so apparently strong, is no match for the returning light, so that now only patches of darkness survive near the ground (since the rising sun is low in the sky). In lines five, six and seven, short, hard sounds produced by alliteration and assonance (particularly the hard 'a' sound) adds to the impression of destruction:

Wake: the vaulted shadow shatters,

Trampled to the floor it spanned,
And the tent of night in tatters

The uneven battle between night and morning is also clear in the contrast between the metaphor of the darkness as a "tent" (small and confining) and the daylight as a pavilion (large and airy). The light covers the land from horizon to horizon.

Each of the first three stanzas opens with a strong imperative ("Wake … Wake … Up, lad, up …"). Orders like these are, of course, appropriate in a military context. The remainder of the poem, however, is rather unmilitary in that it is an argument for getting up and seizing the day. Sergeant majors do not tend to be so philosophical, nor are the arguments specific to military personnel. Man was made to be "a rover." Stanza four uses heavy personification. Both nature and society call on man to roam: "Forelands beacon, [and] belfries call" like encouraging friends; "Towns and countries" call to youth in the same way that a lover invites. Repeating the thought of "Loveliest of Trees," the speaker argues that there is too much world for anyone to see, "Never lad that trod on leather / Lived to feast his heart with all." Life is too short to do and see everything we want to do and see, and therefore there is not a moment to waste in unnecessary "daylight slumber." Once sleep has served the purpose of refreshing the mind and body, it can only hinder a person's destiny – which is to experience life to the full. The aim of life is not merely to experience a lot, in a rather passive way;

the aim is to "to feast [the] heart" – notice the extravagance of the metaphor. Each moment is unique, a perishable commodity, "Breath's a ware that will not keep"; it cannot be stored for later use – use it now or lose it forever! The power of the final stanza is enhanced by the preponderance of strong, single-syllable words. The poem ends by evoking the return of night, when man must "sleep," which symbolizes death, when man will lie "still" as the clay.

This analysis suggests, then, that the military setting implied by the title and in the early stanzas is an extended metaphor. The poem is a call to life – to seize the day precisely because life is short and happiness in life even shorter. Marlow, who likewise does not take literally the military references, suggests a more precise message, "Reveille … is an allegory, and the poet is really thinking of the shortness of time in which he must make his name in scholarship. The travelling must be done in the realms not of gold but of a drearier metal, the piled books of other scholars" (21).

There is, of course, a further level of irony (merely hinted at in the poem) if we entertain the possibility that the soldier, who certainly seems to take some rousing, is dead in his bed.

V

Oh see how thick the goldcup flowers
    Are lying in field and lane,
With dandelions to tell the hours
    That never are told again.
Oh may I squire you round the meads   5
    And pick you posies gay?
– 'Twill do no harm to take my arm.
    "You may, young man, you may."

Ah, spring was sent for lass and lad,
    'Tis now the blood runs gold,   10
And man and maid had best be glad
    Before the world is old.
What flowers to-day may flower to-morrow,
    But never as good as new.
– Suppose I wound my arm right round –   15
    "'Tis true, young man, 'tis true."

Some lads there are, 'tis shame to say,
    That only court to thieve,
And once they bear the bloom away
    'Tis little enough they leave.   20
Then keep your heart for men like me
    And safe from trustless chaps.
My love is true and all for you.
    "Perhaps, young man, perhaps."

Oh, look in my eyes, then, can you doubt?   25
    – Why, 'tis a mile from town.
How green the grass is all about!
    We might as well sit down.
– Ah, life, what is it but a flower?
    Why must true lovers sigh?   30
Be kind, have pity, my own, my pretty, –
    "Good-bye, young man, good-bye."

Notes:

Read "To His Coy Mistress" (c. 1649–60) by Andrew Marvell (1621–1678),
"Comin' Thro' the Rye" (1782) by Robert Burns (1759–96), and "It Was a Lover
and His Lass" (*As You Like It* Act 5 Scene 3) by William Shakespeare (1564-

1616). They also deal with the (attempted) seduction of a maid by a man.

"goldcup" – The bushy shrub St John's Wort is also called 'Gold Cup' because of its golden yellow flowers, 5-6 cm across, but probably the speaker refers to buttercups which grow profusely in meadows.

"dandelions" – These yellow flowering plants are often regarded as weeds. Children "tell the hours" (i.e., count the hours) by using a dandelion clock (i.e., the post-flowering seed bowl). You blow on the bowl until all the seed is blown away, and you count the number of puffs it took – one puff signifies one hour.

"told again" – i.e., counted again, will not come back. Church bells are tolled (a slow, uniform succession of strokes) as a signal of the time or for a funeral. Compare the opening line of "Elegy Written in a Country Churchyard" (1750) by Thomas Gray (1716-1771), "The curfew tolls the knell of parting day."

"squire you round" – i.e., formally escort you around (as a country squire might escort a young lady).

"meads" – i.e., meadows.

"posies" – i.e., small bunches of flowers.

"only court to thieve" – i.e., only court a girl to have sex with her, to steal her virginity.

"bear the bloom away" – i.e., take the girl's virginity.

"but a flower" – i.e., except a flower – that is, life is like a flower in that it also blooms and dies.

Guiding Questions:

1. Identify the two voices in the poem. What do we learn of the situation and character of each speaker?
2. What is important about the season in which the action of the poem is set?
3. With which of the two characters do you feel sympathy? Why?

Final Thoughts

What is new about this poem is that it includes two voices. Seven lines of each stanza are spoken by a young man, and the final line of each by a young woman. The poem tells us virtually nothing about them, except the they are walking together through the flowerful meadows (which suggests that they are 'courting') and that the man is trying to persuade the maid to have sex with him. It is, however, important that the action is set in spring. Spring is traditionally the time for young romance, love and reproduction. In his poem "Loxley Hall" (1842), Alfred Lord Tennyson (1809-1892) wrote, "In the Spring a young man's fancy lightly turns to thoughts of love."

By not individualizing his characters, the poet presents the two antagonists as representative figures: what this ordinary countryman is doing is what men have been doing since the start of time. What is original in Housman's poems is that the young woman proves to be much too smart for the man whose arrogance comes through in what he says. He clearly has not the smallest doubt of success in seducing the girl (and then presumably abandoning her, particularly if she were to become pregnant), but the girl sees through his wheedling arguments and dumps him! Leggett comments, "the naivete of the speaker is exploited in a seduction scene in which his expectations are dashed and his argument is turned against him" (*Poetic Art* 52).

The seduction arguments that the man uses seem to him unanswerable since they are based on our shared knowledge of life's mutability and the inevitability of decline. The present hour, which finds them both in the springtime of life, will never be "told again." Youth is a uniquely precious time when "the blood runs gold." Spring, then, is "sent for lass and lad" as a time of pleasure "before the world is old," meaning both before spring passes and before their prime of life begins to fade. The underlying (unspoken) argument is that it would be to go against Nature not to join in the generation of flora and fauna which they see all around them. The man concedes that the flower that blooms today "may flower to-morrow," but the word "may" implies that one cannot be certain that it will. Yet even if it does, it will never again be just as wonderful as it is right now. (The Greek philosopher Heraclitus [c.535-c.475 BC] said, "No man ever steps in the same river twice, for it's not the same river and he's not the same man.")

The young man now denies that he has any intention of seducing the maid. He takes the moral high-ground condemning as shameful those who steal girls' virginity. He contrasts such "trustless" men with himself whom he portrays as "true" (i.e., honorable) – the alliteration enforces the contrast. Sensing that he is getting nowhere, the man becomes more insistent. Every line of the final stanza is a separate argument, but it is noticeable that the tone had become less rational and more personal and emotional. The exclamations "– Why," and "– Ah," are entirely new (note the importance of the dash); they suggest growing agitation. Finally, he tries emotional blackmail. Why is she making a true lover sigh (i.e., suffer)? He asks rhetorically, implying that the maid is being cruel in denying him. He begs her for "pity" and flatters her by addressing her as "my pretty." The alliteration emphasizes the insincerity of the words – he is playing with words – and the possessive pronoun "my" reveals his deep sense of entitlement. He is not seeing the maid as a person in her own right, as a person the equal of himself.

In the first two stanzas, the young woman seems to accept both the arguments and the actions of the man. She is perfectly willing for him to take her arm and to put his arm around her waist. She concedes that a perfect moment, once lost, can never be recaptured or recreated. However, she is unconvinced by her lover's assertion that he is different from other young chaps. The firm permission in the word "may" and the concurrence in the word "true," are replaced by the conditional, "Perhaps." The poem ends abruptly. Rather than trying to argue the matter, she shows her good sense and independence by telling him firmly,

"Good-bye, young man, good-bye."

The poem is written in four eight-line stanzas, each of which ends in a full stop. This makes each stanza a separate stage in the developing situation. There is a great deal of rhyme in the poem, but no formal rhyme scheme (A B A B A C X X D D D D X E D X C X C X C X E X F H F B X C X X). The varying, inconsistent use of rhyme by the male speaker effectively conveys his wheedling arguments (he literally tries everything), and the fact that the maiden shares none of his rhymes and does not use rhyme herself conveys her independence and assertiveness. The basic meter of the poem is iambic tetrameter though this is used with flexibility to capture the natural speech rhythms of the characters.

In terms of Housman's theme of the transience of pleasure and of life itself, the poem surely carries the message that there are false conclusions to be drawn from true premises: the fact that the bloom will never be so beautiful again is not a valid justification for selfishly destroying the beauty that it has.

VI

When the lad for longing sighs,
   Mute and dull of cheer and pale,
If at death's own door he lies,
   Maiden, you can heal his ail.

Lovers' ills are all to buy: 5
   The wan look, the hollow tone,
The hung head, the sunken eye,
   You can have them for your own.

Buy them, buy them: eve and morn
   Lovers' ills are all to sell.   10
Then you can lie down forlorn;
   But the lover will be well.

Notes:

Read (or listen on YouTube to) the traditional Scottish ballad "Barbara Allen" which tells of the death of a young man slighted in love by the beautiful Barbara. It dates back at least to the mid-eighteenth century.

"heal his ail" – i.e., heal what is ailing him, heal his pain.

"all to buy" – i.e., are all on offer to the young woman, should she choose to take ("buy") them.

Guiding Questions:

1. What exactly ails the young man?
2. How can the young woman cure him of what ails him?
3. What will be the likely consequences for the woman should she do so?

Final Thoughts:

The opening stanza presents a rather conventional, even stereotyped, description of a young man pining away for love of a young woman who has it in her power to heal his pain simply by returning his love. The stanza is full of exaggeration and clichés such as, "at death's own door he lies," which alerts the reader not to take the young man's suffering too seriously. The second stanza continues to emphasize that the man's sorrows are all for the woman, should she choose to accept them, just as she might buy things from a peddler or at a country fair. The speaker urges the woman to, "Buy them, buy them: eve and morn." Note the use of repetition to add emphasis.

So far, the speaker's attitude has been conventional (if we put the clichés and exaggerations of the first stanza down to bad writing), but in the final two lines he adds a twist that alerts the reader to the fact that everything that has been spoken so far has been meant ironically. If the woman buys into the lover's forlorn state, then she will simply change places with him!

The speaker is making the cynical point that for young men seduction is an end in itself; their sole interest in a romance lies in the pursuit. While ever a young man does not get what he wants (sex), he is (or pretends to be) despairing. Yet if, out of pity, the girl allows herself to be seduced, then she cures him of what ails him – not because he will stay with her and live faithfully, but because he is now free to look for someone new to chase – while the woman is left alone in sorrow, perhaps having to deal with the consequences (in the form of pregnancy). What begins apparently as an argument to persuade young women to give their hearts, turn out to be a cautionary tale not to do so.

VII

When smoke stood up from Ludlow,
   And mist blew off from Teme,
And blithe afield to ploughing
   Against the morning beam
I strode beside my team,   5

The blackbird in the coppice
   Looked out to see me stride,
And hearkened as I whistled
   The tramping team beside,
And fluted and replied: 10

"Lie down, lie down, young yeoman;
   What use to rise and rise?
Rise man a thousand mornings
   Yet down at last he lies,
And then the man is wise."   15

I heard the tune he sang me,
   And spied his yellow bill;
I picked a stone and aimed it
   And threw it with a will:
Then the bird was still.   20

Then my soul within me
   Took up the blackbird's strain,
And still beside the horses
   Along the dewy lane
It sang the song again: 25

"Lie down, lie down, young yeoman;
   The sun moves always west;
The road one treads to labour
   Will lead one home to rest,
And that will be the best."   30

Notes:

Read "The Darkling Thrush" (1900) by Thomas Hardy (1840-1928). The 'message' of the thrush in that poem provides an interesting contrast to the 'message' of the blackbird in this poem.

"Teme" – The River Teme rises in mid-Wales and flows south-east. It passes through Ludlow in Shropshire and then into the River Severn.

"blithe" – i.e., happy, without a care in the world.

"the morning beam" – i.e., the slanting beams of the morning sun. The man must therefore be walking east toward the rising sun.

"my team" – i.e., the pair of horses pulling his plough. [In the Middle Ages, oxen were used for plowing because medieval horses in England tended to be small. By the nineteenth century, however, larger breeds of draft horses had been developed for heavy pulling.]

"coppice" – i.e., a small wood where the trees are managed (i.e., periodically cut back to provide wood and to stimulate growth).

"yeoman" – i.e., a man who owns the land that he farms, a freeholder.

Stanza three – Compare, "Vanity of vanities, saith the Preacher, vanity of vanities; all is vanity. What profit hath a man of all his labour which he taketh under the sun? One generation passeth away, and another generation cometh: but the earth abideth for ever. The sun also ariseth, and the sun goeth down, and hasteth to his place where he arose" (*Ecclesiastes* 1:1 King James Version).

Guiding Questions:

1. There are three voices in the poem. Identify each one and say what we learn about them.
2. In what time of the year and at what time of day is the action of the poem set? Why is this important to the theme of the poem?
3. From stanzas three and six, explain precisely the message of the blackbird and the soul's song.
4. What is the effect of the fifth line in each stanza?
5. The poem ends with the words of the blackbird/soul. Does this mean that they constitute the message of the poem?

Final Thoughts:

The setting is a field some miles outside of Ludlow where a young farmer is ploughing his land prior to planting. To state the obvious, given the date, his plough is pulled by a pair of horses. The season is spring, and the time is morning, for the newly lit coal fires in the town are belching out smoke and the farmer is plodding toward the rising sun, which is not yet strong enough to burn off the mists that have collected overnight on the river. The speaker is enjoying his work and the beauty of the setting and whistles to express his careless joy. The sound stimulates a blackbird to whistle back. The speaker says that the bird "replied," a personification that prepares us for the bird's whistling having a very different meaning and message. The poet's choice of a blackbird as the messenger (rather than, say, a sparrow or thrush) is significant. The bird's color obviously suggests

53

death and evil. The bird might symbolize the speaker's own dark subconscious and its message his previously repressed awareness of his own mortality (something that most of us repress most of the time because to continually acknowledge it would be depressing). The description of the ploughing man in stanza two is from the perspective of the bird. Notice the vigor of the verb "stride" which implies self-confidence and vitality, and of the alliterative phrase, "The trampling team," which conveys the power of the horses. These words will contrast with the bird's message.

The blackbird's song carries the message that human life is cyclical: we rise in the morning only to lie down again at night; you are born only to lie down finally in death. This being so the bird asks rhetorically what point there is in the man rising every morning, day after day, when inevitably one must "at last" lie down in death – the words "lie/s" and "down" are each repeated three times for emphasis. In throwing the stone that kills the blackbird, the man is obviously trying to silence the bird's disturbing message. The line, "And threw it with a will," implies not only that the speaker deliberately threw the stone at the bird with the conscious intention of killing it, but more importantly that his conscious mind (his will) sought to reject the bird's song (the message of the unconscious) as untrue. We now see the significance of the earlier detail that the man was "ploughing / Against the morning beam." He was moving east while, as the blackbird tells him, "The sun moves always west." Thus, he was unconsciously trying to defy the passage of time long before the birdsong began – that is, the conflict was in his mind (unacknowledged) from the start. Important too is that the speaker refers to "the blackbird's strain," because it involves a play on words. 'Strain' is a word for the sound of a piece of music, but it also means a state of tension or exhaustion (i.e., stress, anxiety), such as the bird's song causes.

Though he kills the bird in a deliberate act of rebellion against its message, the speaker finds that he has internalized its song and become resigned to its truth. Once the thought of the seeming purposelessness of life has entered his consciousness, he cannot dislodge it. The sun which called him to labor in the morning, "moves always west," and the road on which one sets out each day will inevitably "lead one home to rest" ("home" and "rest" being euphemisms for death). Life is a paradox: the work we do (presumably to improve our lot on earth) will inevitable lead only to our death; the "best" form of rest is death. The poem ends with the song of the blackbird/soul, a declaration of existential *Angst* (the sense of anxiety, despair and hopelessness caused by the conviction that fact of human mortality robs life of all meaning). The poem, however, merely presents the conflict of two views of human activity; it makes no choice between them.

VIII

"Farewell to barn and stack and tree,
    Farewell to Severn shore.
Terence, look your last at me,
    For I come home no more."

"The sun burns on the half-mown hill,   5
    By now the blood is dried;
And Maurice amongst the hay lies still
    And my knife is in his side."

"My mother thinks us long away;
    'Tis time the field were mown.   10
She had two sons at rising day,
    To-night she'll be alone."

"And here's a bloody hand to shake,
    And oh, man, here's good-bye;
We'll sweat no more on scythe and rake,   15
    My bloody hands and I."

"I wish you strength to bring you pride,
    And a love to keep you clean,
And I wish you luck, come Lammastide,
    At racing on the green."   20

"Long for me the rick will wait,
    And long will wait the fold,
And long will stand the empty plate,
    And dinner will be cold."

Notes.

Read this from *Genesis* Chapter 4 (King James Version):

    1. And Adam knew Eve his wife; and she conceived, and bare Cain, and said, I have gotten a man from the Lord.

    2. And she again bare his brother Abel. And Abel was a keeper of sheep, but Cain was a tiller of the ground.

    3. And in process of time it came to pass, that Cain brought of the fruit of the ground an offering unto the Lord.

    4. And Abel, he also brought of the firstlings of his flock and of the fat thereof. And the Lord had respect unto Abel and to his

offering:

5. But unto Cain and to his offering he had not respect. And Cain was very wroth, and his countenance fell.

6. And the Lord said unto Cain, Why art thou wroth? and why is thy countenance fallen?

7. If thou doest well, shalt thou not be accepted? and if thou doest not well, sin lieth at the door. And unto thee shall be his desire, and thou shalt rule over him.

8. And Cain talked with Abel his brother: and it came to pass, when they were in the field, that Cain rose up against Abel his brother, and slew him.

"stack" – i.e., haystack.

"long away" – i.e., the mother is becoming concerned at how long the brothers have been away from home.

"Lammastide" – Lammas Day, August 1st, is a holiday festival celebrating the annual wheat harvest.

"scythe" – i.e., a harvesting tool with a long, curved blade on the end of a long pole attached to two short handles used for cutting down long-stemmed crops like grass or corn.

"rake" – i.e., a harvesting tool with teeth, or tines, for scraping together cut grass, hay, etc.

"rick" – i.e., a stack of hay or straw

"the fold" – i.e., a pen or enclosure in a field for livestock, especially sheep.

Guiding Questions:

1. Who is the speaker? What has he done? What is he planning to do?
2. To whom is the poem addressed?

Final Thoughts:

In the form of a modern ballad, the poet updates the Biblical story of Cain and Abel in which Cain kills his brother out of jealousy and is banished by God and condemned to wander forever about the world. The speaker reflects that after his flight:

> Long for me the rick will wait,
> And long will wait the fold

Evidently, this identifies the speaker, who earlier said, "We'll sweat no more on scythe and rake, / My bloody hands and I" as the farmer, the tiller of the soil, (like Cain) and his brother Maurice as the shepherd (like Abel). Thus, the poem uses myth to establish the archetypal pattern of the loss of innocence and the resulting expulsion from Paradise.

In this poem, the reason for the murder is not given, though it seems to have been an act of sudden passion while the two were mowing a field rather than something that the speaker had planned and carefully thought through. The speaker seems shocked by what he has done and in despair. In stanza one, he enumerates the things that he has lost: his relationship with the land – both the land he farms and the surrounding natural environment; his friendship with Terence; and his home and family. He has made no effort to conceal his crime: Maurice's body still lies in the field, the speaker's bloody knife beside him – though by now the sun will have dried the blood. Though the murderer does not explicitly say so, it is clear that he intends to flee, with the intention of never coming back, leaving his mother at home to mourn. Probably he intends to leave not only Shropshire but England, for if he is arrested, he will face being hanged. Some critics sense that the speaker intends to commit suicide – the ultimate evasion – but there is no actual suggestion of this.

The theme of the poem is the loss of innocence. The speaker has shattered the Eden-like setting of rural Shropshire by the murder he has committed and must live now in guilt and fear. He has left a "half-mown hill" a phrase heavy in metaphorical meaning. It indicates both that he has killed his only brother (the other half of himself since he tells us that his mother "had two sons at rising day") and that he has destroyed his own life half way through. He tells us that his brother, "Maurice amongst the hay lies still," and this too has metaphorical meaning for hay is cut grass. It is lying dead and drying in the sun just as is Maurice, who has returned to the dust from which he sprang. There is a sad irony in his statement, "My mother thinks us long away." The mother of the two boys is by now puzzled that her sons have not returned since they should have finished their mowing, but both are, in reality, much farther away than she can know because one is dead and the other is determined to become an exile. She will never see either of them alive again.

In the last three stanzas of the poem, the speaker concentrates again upon the things that he has lost by his crime. No more will he labor in the fields alongside his friend Terence; unlike his friend, he can look forward to no love to keep him "clean"; he will have no part in the festivals and games of the community; he will never see his beloved farm again; and at home his place will be forever vacant and dinner will always be cold.

The poem is written in quatrains with the traditional ballad rhyme scheme (A B A B). Its theme is again that of a mortal man who, by his own action, ruins what little chance of temporary happiness the human condition allows.

IX

On moonlit heath and lonesome bank
   The sheep beside me graze;
And yon the gallows used to clank
   Fast by the four cross ways.

A careless shepherd once would keep   5
   The flocks by moonlight there,
And high amongst the glimmering sheep
   The dead man stood on air

They hang us now in Shrewsbury jail:
   The whistles blow forlorn,   10
And trains all night groan on the rail
   To men that die at morn.

There sleeps in Shrewsbury jail to-night,
   Or wakes, as may betide,
A better lad, if things went right,   15
   Than most that sleep outside.

And naked to the hangman's noose
   The morning clocks will ring
A neck God made for other use
   Than strangling in a string.   20

And sharp the link of life will snap,
   And dead on air will stand
Heels that held up as straight a chap
   As treads upon the land.

So here I'll watch the night and wait   25
   To see the morning shine,
When he will hear the stroke of eight
   And not the stroke of nine;

And wish my friend as sound a sleep
   As lads' I did not know,   30
That shepherded the moonlit sheep
   A hundred years ago.

Notes:

Housman's own note on this poem – Line 7: "Hanging in chains was called keeping sheep by moonlight."
"Fast by the four cross ways" – Until 1868, hangings in England were performed in public. Gallows were frequently placed where two roads crossed and the bodies of murderers were often buried there. This may have been done to confuse the spirit of the executed person which would have trouble deciding which way to go.
"Shrewsbury jail" – The first Shrewsbury Prison was built in 1793. It was completely rebuilt in 1877. It is located close Shrewsbury railway station and junction as mentioned in the poem.
"as may betide" – i.e., as chance might have it.
"dead on air will stand" – A graphic oxymoron describing the hanged man suspended in mid-air.
"As lads' I" – i.e., as the sleep of lads (hence the possessive apostrophe).

Guiding Question:

1. Describe the setting. What time is it? Where is the speaker? What is he doing? What is nearby?
2. Who is at this moment in Shrewsbury jail? Why? How does the speaker feel about this person's fate?
3. Comment on the significance of the pronouns in the line, "They hang us now in Shrewsbury jail."
4. How does the poet make the lines that describe the act of being hung particularly effective?
5. How long is the speaker going to stay where he is? Why?

Final Thoughts

The speaker is in reflective mood. It is night, and he is at a place where shepherds used to tend their sheep as they grazed in the moonlight. He recalls that he is near to the crossroads where the gallows used to stand before all hangings were done in Shrewsbury jail and reflects that many a "careless shepherd" hung at that place surrounded, as is the speaker, by grazing sheep. Now the condemned men are in Shrewsbury jail where their final night on earth is disturbed by the sound of the trains. The "clank" of the gallows has been replaced by the "forlorn" whistles and ceaseless "groan" of the railway engines, as though wailing for the death of the man – such is the measure of progress. What is unchanged is the victim-status of those who are hanged: in their case, the short span of human life is shown in its extreme form since it is measured in hours and minutes – existence for them ends before the stroke of nine. "They hang us now in Shrewsbury jail," he says. The unidentified "They" presumably

59

represents the authorities who exploit their power over the common people – the "us" with whom the speaker identifies.

In stanza four, the speaker gets to the real point: that very night, either asleep or awake, lies someone he knows who will die in the morning. The irony is that the speaker says that this person is, "A better lad, if things went right, / Than most that sleep outside." Not only is the condemned person very young, but the speaker claims that he is a victim of circumstances – though he never elaborates on this. Hanging such a person seems to be going against the will of God who made the young man's neck "for other use / Than strangling in a string." Note the macabre play on the word "ring": the morning clocks will chime the hour of eight, and the convict's neck will be wrung. The alliteration of the long 's' sound together with the long vowels really conveys the moment when the noose is tightened around the victim's neck. The next line is an abrupt contrast, "And sharp the link of life will snap." Here the words are all monosyllables and the vowels are short as is the alliteration of the 'l' sound and the 's' sound. The reader almost feels the man's neck breaking! The speaker repeats the idea that a hanged man "dead on air will stand." This is an oxymoron (you cannot stand on nothing) which encapsulates the unnatural nature of capital punishment.

Finally, in stanza seven, we understand why the speaker is in the fields this night: he wants to be far away from the jail at the moment of execution. His final wish is that the condemned man will sleep as soundly in death as did the young men (by implication lads just as much a victim of circumstances as him) who were hung on the gallows by the crossroads, "A hundred years ago." Execution by hanging has become a metaphor for the fate of everyman. Just as the speaker identifies with the condemned man – a man inherently "better" than others but the victim of "things" beyond his control – so the reader is invited to see his own fate in that of the hanged man.

"[N]ever send to know for whom the bell tolls; it tolls for thee," writes John Donne (1572-1631) (*Devotions Upon Emergent Occasions, Meditation XVII*).

X   *MARCH*

The sun at noon to higher air,
Unharnessing the silver Pair
That late before his chariot swam,
Rides on the gold wool of the Ram.

So braver notes the storm-cock sings   5
To start the rusted wheel of things,
And brutes in field and brutes in pen
Leap that the world goes round again.

The boys are up the woods with day
To fetch the daffodils away,   10
And home at noonday from the hills
They bring no dearth of daffodils.

Afield for palms the girls repair,
And sure enough the palms are there,
And each will find by hedge or pond   15
Her waving silver-tufted wand.

In farm and field through all the shire
The eye beholds the heart's desire;
Ah, let not only mine be vain,
For lovers should be loved again.   20

Notes:

Read "I Wandered Lonely as a Cloud" (c.1804) by William Wordsworth (1770-1850) if only because it also mentions, "A host, of golden daffodils."

Search YouTube for "Snow Falls' Albion Band." The song captures brilliantly the transition from winter to spring in the countryside.

"the silver Pair" – In Greek mythology, Selene (sister of the sun-god Helios) is the goddess of the moon who drives her moon chariot across the heavens. Selene's silver chariot has two snow-white horses.

"the gold wool of the Ram" – Khrysomallos, a fabulous, flying, golden-fleeced ram became the constellation Aries. (His golden fleece was the goal of Jason and the Argonauts.)

"storm-cock" – i.e., the mistle thrush, a large, European thrush so called because it feeds on the berries of the mistletoe.

"palms … waving silver-tufted wand" – There is evidently a reference in the use of the word "palms" to the description of Christ's entry into Jerusalem on Palm

Sunday, which sometimes falls in the latter part of March:

> 12. On the next day much people that were come to the feast, when they heard that Jesus was coming to Jerusalem,
>
> 13. Took branches of palm trees, and went forth to meet him, and cried, Hosanna: Blessed is the King of Israel that cometh in the name of the Lord. (*John* 12 King James Version)

"The flowering shoots of pussy willow are used both in Europe and America for spring religious decoration on Palm Sunday, as a replacement for palm branches, which do not grow that far north" (Wikipedia contributors. "Pussy willow." *Wikipedia, The Free Encyclopedia*. Wikipedia, The Free Encyclopedia, 3 Oct. 2019. Web. 18 Nov. 2019.). This is are the wands to which the speaker is referring.

Guiding Question:

1. Having reached its highest point in the sky at noon, what more does the sun want? How does it achieve its desire?
2. What do the animals described in stanza two want and what do they do to achieve it?
3. For what are the boys and the girls searching in the woods and fields?
4. What does the speaker want?
5. What moral does he draw from the examples of the sun, the animals, and the boys and girls he has described?

Final Thoughts:

The first quatrain describes the noon in complex astrological terms derived from Greek mythology. The idea is, however, simple: having reached its zenith, the sun aspires to go still higher than the silver chariot of Selene can take it and rides instead upon the gold fleece of Aries. The second stanza turns to more everyday creatures that show the same ambition. The song of the thrush and the leaping of the farm animals in their pens are each trying to "start the rusted wheel of things" as winter gives way to spring and thus make sure that "the world goes round again." Similarly, the boys gathering daffodils (which bloom in late winter and early spring) in the woods at dawn return with bunches and bunches at noon. And the girls search the fields for "palms" and each will find their "waving silver-tufted wand," a metaphor that suggests the magic of the season of rebirth which is related to the resurrection of Christ. The relevance of the title is now evident for in March the year begins to revolve again after the long sleep of winter.

The final stanza clearly expresses the moral of the poem: everything in the speaker's experience illustrates "the heart's desire" being fulfilled – even exceeded. He therefore prays that he should not be the sole exception because "lovers should be loved again" – that is, the love they feel for someone should be returned.

XI

On your midnight pallet lying
    Listen, and undo the door:
Lads that waste the light in sighing
    In the dark should sigh no more;
Night should ease a lover's sorrow;
Therefore, since I go to-morrow;   5
    Pity me before.

In the land to which I travel,
    The far dwelling, let me say –
Once, if here the couch is gravel,
    In a kinder bed I lay,   10
And the breast the darnel smothers
Rested once upon another's
    When it was not clay.

Notes:

Go to YouTube and search for the song "I'm a Rover" of which you will find many versions. This traditional ballad deals with the same situation of a young man seeking to be let into his beloved's bed at midnight.
"pallet" – i.e., a humble form of bed made of straw or hay.
"couch" – i.e., bed.
"darnel" – A type of ryegrass that grows as a weed in wheat fields. It often hosts a fungus that is intoxicating and even poisonous to humans and animals.

Guiding Questions:

1. Describe the setting of the poem.
2. Where is the speaker going the next day? Why?
3. What arguments does the speaker use to persuade the person he loves to open the door to her/his bedroom and let him in? Do the arguments succeed?

Final Thoughts:

This is a seduction poem. The speaker is literally outside the bedroom door of the person he loves arguing for admittance. His arguments are general (lads who spend the day sighing for love should not also have to sigh all night since night is the time for lovers to be together) and specific (this is the speaker's last night before he goes away). There is plenty of emotional blackmail. The speaker tells his love that if he finds abroad/in death that his "couch is gravel," he will want to remember that just once before he left, "In a kinder bed" he lay. When he feels himself lying on the darnel that smothers his longing, he wants to be able to remember that he once laid his breast upon the one he loved, "When it was not clay." This I take to mean when it also had feelings, unlike clay which has none. This implies that the lover's journey is a metaphor for death and that his plea is for love to be returned because once this brief life is ended it never can be reciprocated.

Whether these arguments succeed in softening the beloved's heart, we do not know. Precisely why the speaker is going away, we are not told. The gender of the beloved is never specified. As with all of Housman's love poetry what we clearly identify as gay love, the Victorians either naively assumed to be heterosexual love or allowed themselves to believe it to be so.

XII

When I watch the living meet,
   And the moving pageant file
Warm and breathing through the street
   Where I lodge a little while,

If the heats of hate and lust   5
   In the house of flesh are strong,
Let me mind the house of dust
   Where my sojourn shall be long.

In the nation that is not
   Nothing stands that stood before;   10
There revenges are forgot,
   And the hater hates no more;

Lovers lying two and two
   Ask not whom they sleep beside,
And the bridegroom all night through   15
   Never turns him to the bride.

Notes:

Read "Ode to a Grecian Urn" (1819) by John Keats (1795-1821). One of the panels on the urn depicts the same sort of frozen love as the final quatrain of Housman's poem:
    Bold Lover, never, never canst thou kiss,
    Though winning near the goal – yet, do not grieve;
    She cannot fade, though thou hast not thy bliss,
    For ever wilt thou love, and she be fair! (lines 17–20)
"the moving pageant file" – Formal pageants involving processions through the streets of a town would have been quite common at festival times such as Easter. However, here the term is metaphorical: the speaker is observing the pageant of life, the normal comings and goings of people in the street.
"mind" – i.e., remember.
"sojourn" – i.e., stay.
"the nation that is not" – i.e. among the dead, an oxymoron because a "nation" in the underworld is no nation at all.
"turns him" – i.e., turns himself.

Guiding Questions:

1.What are the characteristics of the life he sees around him that the speaker mentions in the first two stanzas?

2. Comment on the significance of the words "lodge" and "sojourn" in the contexts in which they are used.

3. In the poem "To his Coy Mistress" Andrew Marvel writes, "The grave's a fine and private place, / But none, I think, do there embrace." Is that also the message of this poem?

Final Thoughts:

Stanza one opens with the speaker as an observer of life. We can visualize him looking out on the life of the town perhaps from the window of his lodgings. However, the statement, "Where I lodge a little while," is more importantly metaphorical: the house in which his consciousness resides is the human body. The speaker is aware of how temporary his life is – it will soon come to an end. Stanza two contrasts the strong "hate and lust" that he feels and observes in others with their absence in "the house of dust." He uses the word "sojourn" to describe his time being dead. This is intentionally and bitterly ironic since the word normally means a short or temporary stay. Its use impresses on the reader the truth that while life is, indeed, brief, death is eternal (particularly to a writer like Housman who had no faith in the Christian promise of resurrection).

Death wipes out everything, "Nothing stands that stood before." Death is the great oxymoron, "the nation that is not" – note the harsh alliteration. Neither hatred nor love survive there, but of these two the speaker is more concerned with the loss of the latter, "the bridegroom all night through / Never turns him to the bride." In death the lovers' state, caught at its moment of greatest intensity, can never be altered by the decay of time. In this they are fortunate, but paradoxically in death their love can never again be consummated and in this lies their tragedy.

The poem is, then, a *memento mori*. Far from being pessimistic, it is a warning to appreciate "moving … / Warm and breathing" while we experience them. It is a warning even to avoid, "the heats of hate and lust," because they too will soon be gone forever: life is too short to allow them to take up a moment. Value and return love, the speaker is saying, in the here-and-now, because not to do so is to fail to make the most of life's potential.

XIII

When I was one-and-twenty
  I heard a wise man say,
"Give crowns and pounds and guineas
  But not your heart away;
Give pearls away and rubies   5
  But keep your fancy free."
But I was one-and-twenty,
  No use to talk to me.

When I was one-and-twenty
  I heard him say again,   10
"The heart out of the bosom
  Was never given in vain;
'Tis paid with sighs a plenty
  And sold for endless rue."
And I am two-and-twenty,   15
  And oh, 'tis true, 'tis true.

Notes:

Read the poem "Down by the Salley Gardens" (1889) by William Butler Yeats (1865-1939) which has a similar theme of advice about love being not taken.

"crowns and pounds and guineas" – In pre-decimal days, British currency was based on the Pound Sterling. There were twenty shillings in a pound and twelve pence in a shilling. A crown was a coin worth five shillings, and a guinea was a coin worth twenty-one shillings.

"'keep your fancy free'" – i.e., do not get too attached to one person, keep your affections free.

"bosom" – This is the only end-of-line word that does not rhyme with any others.

"in vain" – i.e., for nothing, at no personal cost.

"rue" – i.e., regret, remorse, sorrow.

Guiding Questions:

1. What can the reader infer about the "wise man" whose advice the speaker heard a year ago?
2. What advice did this man offer to the young men to whom he was speaking?
3. How did the speaker feel about that advice at the time? How does he feel about it now?
4. Account for the change in his views.

Final Thoughts:

In this 'innocence-to-experience' lyric, the twenty-two-year-old speaker is reflecting back on the fool he was just a year before when he received good advice about not falling in love. He failed to heed this advice and now knows what doing so has cost him.

In stanza one, the reader learns that the advice came from a "wise man," a judgment with the benefit of hindsight. About this man, we learn nothing more, nor are we told of the circumstances under which the speaker "heard" what he was saying, although the use of that word suggests that the man might not have been speaking one-on-one to the speaker. We can also infer that the "man" was older than the speaker and that his wisdom came from him already having suffered the pain of which he speaks. His advice was that young men should never "give [their] heart[s] away" by falling in love with one person. He told them they could give away money and jewels, but that they must at all costs keep their "fancy" – that is, not give their heart away. This probably sounded pretty cynical to the idealistic young man who reflects sadly that he "was one-and-twenty, [and it was] / No use to talk to me," because he did not heed the warning.

In stanza two, the speaker remembers that the man went on to say that the heart is never given to another person without some cost or consequences. There is always emotional suffering and bitter regret, but the damage has been done. The young speaker reflects that he did not follow this sage advice. The reader infers that he allowed himself to become entangled by giving away his heart to someone who did not return his feelings. Now, a mere year later, with reference to the older man's advice, experience has taught him "oh, 'tis true, 'tis true." Too late, he realizes that he should have listened, for the realization of the transitory nature of love has been a shocking epiphany that has almost destroyed him. Ironically, he has become the older man as the result of his own experiences.

If the ostensible theme of the poem is that the young should always heed the wisdom of experience and never give the heart away because it will cost too much in emotional pain and sorrow, then that theme is undercut by the way in which the speaker presents it. The wise man comes across as cynical and defeatist. That is probably why the speaker ignored his advice and began the cycle of loving and suffering again. Everyone – the wise man, the speaker and (perhaps even) the reader – has to make this mistake for themselves, and it is perhaps a good thing too if the only way to avoid having one's feelings hurt is to stop feeling! It is one thing to know what the wise thing to do is, but it is an altogether different matter to actually do it.

The poem is a dramatic monologue (i.e., a story told in the first person by the protagonist) written in the form of a Scottish lyric ballad. It has two rhymed stanzas of eight lines; the rhyme scheme is A B C B C D A D in the first stanza and A B C B A D A D in the second stanza. All of the even-numbered lines contain perfect or full end rhymes (i.e., after their different opening consonants they contain identical, accented vowel and consonant sounds) such as "say" and "away," but the odd-numbered lines, though they do sometimes rhyme, have no set rhyme scheme. Each of the even-numbered lines contains six syllables (iambic triameter), but each of the odd-numbered lines contains seven syllables (creating what is called a feminine ending, that is, there is an extra, unaccented syllable at the end of the line). The stanzas are broken in half by heavy end-line punctuation and by the rhyming of the second and fourth lines of each. Short vowel sounds predominate as does monosyllabic diction (seventy-six of ninety words are monosyllables). Gordon Lea, commenting on these features of the verse contends that they, "combine merrily to undermine the sadness of the speaker, a rejected or abandoned lover" (74).

XIV

There pass the careless people
    That call their souls their own:
Here by the road I loiter,
    How idle and alone.

Ah, past the plunge of plummet,   5
    In seas I cannot sound,
My heart and soul and senses,
    World without end, are drowned.

His folly has not fellow
    Beneath the blue of day   10
That gives to man or woman
    His heart and soul away.

There flowers no balm to sain him
    From east of earth to west
That's lost for everlasting   15
    The heart out of his breast.

Here by the labouring highway
    With empty hands I stroll:
Sea-deep, till doomsday morning,
    Lie lost my heart and soul.   20

Notes:

"careless" – i.e., without concerns or worries.

"plummet" – The word is here a noun not a verb. A "plummet" is a stone or metal weight (called a plum or plum bob) attached to a line that is used to indicate vertical measurement. A similar device, a sounding line, was used to measure the depth of water under a ship or boat. The line had marks on it indicating the depth in fathoms when the lead weight touched the bottom of the river or the sea.

"sound" – i.e., find the bottom of.

"World without end" – The phrase comes from the King James Version of the *Bible*, "But Israel shall be saved in the LORD with an everlasting salvation: ye shall not be ashamed nor confounded world without end" (*Isiah* 45.17), and "Unto him be glory in the church by Christ Jesus throughout all ages, world without end. Amen." (*Ephesians* 3.21).

"blue of day" – i.e., beneath the sun.

"There flowers no balm to sain him" – A "balm" is a healing salve or ointment.

To "sain" is to make the sign of the Cross over someone to bless or to heal him. Compare, "Is there no balm in Gilead; is there no physician there?" (*Jeremiah* 8:22, King James Version).

Guiding Questions:

1. Who are the people over "There"? Who is the person over "Here"? How do the two sets differ?
2. In stanza two, the speaker says he has plunged into the sea from a great height and drowned. Explain what he means by this extended metaphor.
3. There is more alliteration in lines 5-10 than in any other set of six lines. Comment on how alliteration adds to the meaning of these lines.
4. What is the "folly [that] has no fellow"?
5. There is a great deal of religious language in this poem. Find examples. Why does the poet use words with religious connotations?
6. What do you understand by the unusual phrase "the labouring highway"?
7. Why does the speaker have empty hands?

Final Thoughts:

The first stanza contains two contrasting adverbs: "There" and "Here." These divide the stanza into equal halves: the first two lines describe people in general and the second the individual speaker who sees himself as being distinct from them. Two contrasting verbs are used to describe these different sets: "pass" and "loiter." The first verb suggests the motion of the "careless people" who remain free because they have not committed their "souls" to loving another person. There is a clever play on the word "careless," for in a real sense there are the careful ones, the ones who take no chances in life by not loving, and as a result they avoid suffering (care). These people think that they make their own decisions and clearly believe that their lives have a sense of direction, but the verb "pass" qualifies their supposed autonomy: it implies that they are in reality, purposeless. The second verb, "loiter," describes the speaker. It implies that he is trapped in a state of stasis; if the others are fooling themselves, he is at least honest in acknowledging that his life is directionless. The word "loiter" certainly has negative connotations of aimlessness. As yet the reader does not know why, unlike the mass of people whom he sees going about their lives, the speaker recognizes himself as being "idle and alone."

The explanation comes in the second stanza; it is expressed in an extended metaphor. The speaker feels like one who has thrown himself into a sea whose bottom he cannot find and whose "heart and soul and senses" are "drowned." Stanza two is rich in alliteration – it occurs in each line. The short 'p' sounds in line five capture the suddenness and violence of his fall, while in the remaining lines the long 's' and 'w' sounds convey his sense of being lost in a great ocean.

The phrase "world without end" has religious connotations. It suggests that the speaker is lost in an eternity of sorrow.

Stanza three returns the focus to the speaker who calls loving a "folly" beyond all of the errors that man can make. Note the harsh short 'f' and 'b' alliteration in lines 9-10. Reading the poem, you can hear the speaker's anger and bitterness against his fate. In the next stanza, he tells us that there is no remedy, either medicinal or spiritual, for the condition of one who has given away his heart to another. Such a person (and he speaks from experience) is lost.

The final stanza repeats the contrast of the first between the solitary speaker and the crowd of humanity. They travel on the "labouring highway," an example of a transferred epithet; that is, the modifier or epithet is transferred from the noun it is meant to describe (the others) to another noun in the sentence (the road). The phrase suggests that these people actually perform some function while the speaker's hands are "empty" because he does not. However, the highway is also a metaphor for life itself which is inherently laborsome. In contrast to the others on the "highway," the speaker is "Sea-deep." He is too depressed to do any work or to take any active role in life. He will merely "stroll" through life – a drowned man in a bottomless sea, forever. In this way, how the speaker expresses himself appears to undercut what he seems to be wanting to say, or claim, about himself.

XV

Look not in my eyes, for fear
    They mirror true the sight I see,
And there you find your face too clear
    And love it and be lost like me.
One the long nights through must lie   5
    Spent in star-defeated sighs,
But why should you as well as I
    Perish? gaze not in my eyes.

A Grecian lad, as I hear tell,
    One that many loved in vain,   10
Looked into a forest well
    And never looked away again.
There, when the turf in springtime flowers,
    With downward eye and gazes sad,
Stands amid the glancing showers   15
    A jonquil, not a Grecian lad.

Notes:

"star-defeated" – This recalls the description of Romeo and Juliet as "A pair of star-crossed lovers" (Act 1 Prologue). Astrologically speaking, their love is "death-marked" by the position of the stars at the time of their births. Similarly, the speaker feels that his love is destined by the stars not to be returned.
"Grecian lad" – In Greek mythology, Narcissus, son of the river god Cephissus and the nymph Liriope, was a hunter. Because of his beauty, many fell in love with him, but he proudly rejected them. One such was a nymph who sorrowfully roamed around the woods for the rest of her life following his rejection. To punish Narcissus, Nemesis, the goddess of retribution and revenge, led him to a pool; there, the handsome young man saw his reflection in the water and fell in love with it. When he understood what had happened and that his love was hopeless, he fell into despair and committed suicide.
"jonquil" – Commonly called the rush daffodil, this is a species of Narcissus that flowers in late spring.

Guiding Questions:

1. Explain why the speaker warns the person he loves against looking into his eyes.
2. What did Narcissus lose by falling in love with his own reflection?

Final Thoughts:

This is one of Housman's most obviously homosexual poems because the beloved is compared with Narcissus. Stanza one opens with a mock warning: the person addressed should not look into the speaker's eyes lest he fall in love with his own reflection mirrored there and "be lost" as is the speaker in a hopeless passion. Ostensibly, the speaker's motive is to protect the beloved from lying sleepless every night sighing hopelessly. However, the reader can hardly avoid the unspoken implication that the beloved is superficial, self-involved and entirely lacking in sympathy for the speaker's feelings. Love seems almost trapped at the level of sensual excitation.

The second stanza references the story of Narcissus who became so absorbed in the beauty of his own reflection that he turned into a flower thus losing his humanity. Equating the beloved with Narcissus, "One that many loved in vain," serves further to emphasize the egocentric vanity of the beloved. By comparing his own eyes to the "forest well" into which the Grecian lad stared, the speaker implies that love is a trap, an indication of man's sensual nature. The danger is that allowing oneself to love in this way risks abandoning one's fullest humanity. "In Freudian psychiatry and psychoanalysis, the term narcissism denotes an excessive degree of self-esteem or self-involvement, a condition that is usually a form of emotional immaturity" (The Editors of *Encyclopaedia Britannica*). Sigmund Freud (1856-1939) was not, however, the first person to make this association.

The detail of a "forest well" is a marked divergence from the Narcissus myth in which the Greek lad looks into a forest stream. To state the obvious, wells are deeper than streams and much harder to extricate yourself from if you happen to fall into one! This seems to be Housman's point. The speaker is warning his beloved not to lose his humanity. Notice that in referencing the "forest well," he is playing on the wording of his earlier rhetorical question, "why should you as well as I / Perish?" Housman lets the reader know that is precisely what the speaker has allowed to happen by falling for superficial attraction.

XVI

It nods and curtseys and recovers
    When the wind blows above,
The nettle on the graves of lovers
    That hanged themselves for love.

The nettle nods, the wind blows over,   5
    The man, he does not move,
The lover of the grave, the lover
    That hanged himself for love.

Notes:

The Church did not formerly grant burial in consecrated ground to someone who committed suicide. The grave in this poem appears to be untended and the ground to have reverted to nature.

Guiding Questions:

1. What connotations do the three verbs in line one have for you?
2. What does the wind symbolize?
3. Comment on the significance of calling the dead man a "lover of the grave."

Final Thoughts:

The first line of the poem is deliberately deceptive. The three verbs suggest delicate, formal dance movements (to 'recover' in dance is to return to one's previous position). The second line makes it clear that what is being described is a plant moving in the wind, but the previous association with dance leads the reader to expect that plant to be a beautiful flower. Having thus manipulated the reader's expectations, line three hits us with the truth: what is moving is no flower but a stinging weed growing on the grave of a dead lover. As though this were not shock enough, line four informs us that the grave is that of people, "That hanged themselves for love." The second stanza further draws the contrast between the "lover in the grave" who "does not move" and the nettle and the wind that seem to be in constant motion while the wind blows. Notice how line five recaps, in concentrated form, lines one and two. The phrase "wind blows over" contains ambiguity. Does it mean that the nettle nods constantly because the wind always blows, or that the nettle bows until the wind dies down (i.e., by being adaptable and flexible, the nettle survives)?

The poem thus explores the human predicament: man is mortal in an immortal natural world. The wind represents the suffering to which all life must be subject. The pernicious nettle can recover from its buffeting, but the man, who metaphorically felt its sting in the form of unrequited love, cannot. Notice how the lover has changed. He is no longer one who hanged himself for love; he is now described as one who took his own life because he was in love with the idea of death. The "lover of the grave" has by suicide won a victory over the pain and buffeting of life (symbolized by the nettle and the wind). In the words of John Keats, suicidal lovers having suffered the buffets of unrequited love become "in love with easeful Death" ("Ode to a Nightingale").

F. W. Bateson comments on the closing line:

> The last line of the second stanza is not, as careless reading might suggest, a repetition of the first stanza's last line but a contrast to it: the plurals have become singulars. The lovers of the first stanza may have died together in a suicide pact, but the second stanza presents a solitary suicide, a single rejected or abandoned lover. ("The Poetry of Emphasis," in Ricks Ed. 139)

Whether love is mutual or unrequited, the decision to love appears to issue a challenge to human mortality, to claim a permanence, and inflexibility, that is inherently self-destructive given the human condition.

In commenting on the symbolism of the nettle, I can do no better than quote the comments of Randall Jarrell:

> [The nettle] stands for the hurting and inescapable conditions of life, the prosperous (but sympathetically presented and almost admiringly accepted) evil of the universe ... The nettle is merely repeating above the grave, compelled by the wind, what the man in the grave did once, when the wind blew through him. So living is (we must take it as being) just a repetition of little meaningless nodding actions, actions that haven't even the virtue of being our own – since the wind forces them out of us; life as the maker [,] man as the tree or nettle helpless and determined. ("Texts From Housman" in Ricks Ed. 57-58)

In ballads roses are intimately connected to lovers. On their graves, the rose symbolizes remembrance, but here Housman substitutes the nettle which symbolizes "forgetfulness ... All the nettle's actions emphasize its indifference and removedness ... the nettle above the grave is alone, inhuman and casual, the representative of a nature indifferent to man (*Ibid.* 59).

That said, there is an entirely different way of interpreting the symbolism of the nettle, as A. W. Bateson argues:

> [T]he nettle seems to stand too for the gracefulness and resilience of a living object. In the series of verbs with which the poem opens – each verb on syllable longer than its predecessor as the force of the wind increases – the nettle adjusts itself to the pressure of external circumstance by its mobility. Unlike the suicide who "does not move," who is finished physically, the

nettle survives and in due course "the wind blows over." ("The
Poetry of Emphasis," in Ricks Ed. 140)

Notice that the lovers are first plural then singular, but that the nettle is singular throughout. Survival lies in detachment. Also, the nettle lacks consciousness: it may well be buffeted about by the wind, but it does not suffer psychologically from what the Murderer in Macbeth calls "the vile blows and buffets of the world" (Act 3 Scene 1).

XVII

Twice a week the winter thorough
   Here stood I to keep the goal:
Football then was fighting sorrow
   For the young man's soul.

Now in May time to the wicket   5
   Out I march with bat and pad:
See the son of grief at cricket
   Trying to be glad.

Try I will; no harm in trying:
   Wonder 'tis how little mirth   10
Keeps the bones of man from lying
   On the bed of earth.

Notes:

Read "Ode on Melancholy" (1819) by John Keats (1795-1821) to see how a great poet deals with existential despair.

In England, soccer is played in late autumn, winter and early spring; cricket is played in late spring, summer and early autumn. British schools have always seen sports as an important part of boys' education, helping to build *mens sana in corpore sano* (i.e., a healthy mind in a healthy body).

"Thorough" – An old spelling of "through."

"Football" – i.e., soccer.

"no harm in trying" – A common British aphorism with various forms – 'Can't blame a man for trying!'

Guiding Questions:

1. Why did the speaker play soccer and cricket?
2. In stanza three he says he will, "Try ... no harm in trying." Try what?

Final Thoughts:

The speaker looks out over his local recreation (i.e., sports) ground. It is summer and the goalposts have been removed, but he identifies exactly where he stood twice a week in winter playing goalkeeper for the local football team. At this moment, he is striding out to bat for his local cricket team. In winter, he played to fight off his melancholy "sorrow," and still in summer he plays to try to overcome his depression and "be glad."

No reason is given for the speaker's sorrow, but Housman uses the football and cricket seasons to show that it lasts throughout the year. He is, however, determined to keep trying to ward off his sadness. The speaker's determination comes across in his choice of position in soccer: the goalkeeper is the last line of defense, and it takes a lot of courage. His resolution to "keep the goal" symbolizes his determination to keep depression at bay. There is a play on the word "goal" which is both the net in soccer and the man's determination to beat 'the blues.' Similarly, he "march[es]" out to bat, suggesting someone willing to do battle to protect his wicket, which symbolizes his life. The same resolution is evident in the repetition of "Trying ... Try ... trying." Realistic enough to know that his success may be limited, he also knows there is "no harm in trying." Because after all, he says, it is a wonder "how little mirth," how little enjoyment in life, keeps a person from just giving up on living entirely, and becoming merely dead bones lying in the earth.

The poem ends on an ironic note: reflecting on his own experience, the speaker concludes that it takes surprisingly little pleasure in life to make a person want to keep living. Football and cricket stand as symbols for all of the little activities that give humans pleasure and hold back existential angst. This is hardly ringing optimism, but it is rather typically British. Remember the World War II maxim, "Keep calm and carry on."

It seems only fair to present an entirely different reading of the poem. Edith Sitwell commented acidly, "If he means us to understand that cricket, and cricket alone, has prevented men from committing suicide, then their continuation on this earth seems hardly worthwhile" (quoted in Firchow et al. 21-22). But then, so far as I am aware, Dame Edith Sitwell never played cricket, so how would she know?

XVIII

Oh, when I was in love with you,
   Then I was clean and brave,
And miles around the wonder grew
   How well did I behave.

And now the fancy passes by,   5
   And nothing will remain,
And miles around they'll say that I
   Am quite myself again.

Guiding Questions:

1. What transformation in his own conduct does the speaker attribute to his having fallen first in and then out of love?
2. How would you describe the tone of this poem?

Final Thoughts:

Housman has the reputation of being a humorless chap. Certainly *A Shropshire Lad* seems to be full of depressing poems about young men dying before their time, unrequited love, depression, etc. However, some of those who knew him reported that Housman had a wicked sense of humor – as an undergraduate he did, after all, co-found a satirical magazine. That comes to the surface in this short poem in which the lovelorn speaker takes a comic swipe at himself.

The tense of the first line is important since (unlike many of the poems we have read before) the speaker is putting his love firmly in the past. Far from having made him sad, his love made him a better person: "clean[er] and brave[r]" and better "behave[d]." People wondered at the transformation! The idea that love made him braver is conventional enough, but that it made him wash more thoroughly and conduct himself better are hardly responses the reader associates with love. He is able to laugh at the effect of his being "in love" because he now recognizes that it was only a "fancy" that has passed: he is, as we say now, so 'over it' that "nothing will remain." The joke is that everyone notices the change. The speaker is back to being the dirty, cowardly, badly behaved lad he was before the made the mistake of thinking he was in love. The phrase "quite myself" is a lovely comic understatement since his former self was obviously rather disreputable.

XIX *TO AN ATHLETE DYING YOUNG*

The time you won your town the race
We chaired you through the market-place;
Man and boy stood cheering by,
And home we brought you shoulder-high.

To-day, the road all runners come,   5
Shoulder-high we bring you home,
And set you at your threshold down,
Townsman of a stiller town

Smart lad, to slip betimes away
From fields where glory does not stay   10
And early though the laurel grows
It withers quicker than the rose.

Eyes the shady night has shut
Cannot see the record cut,
And silence sounds no worse than cheers   15
After earth has stopped the ears:

Now you will not swell the rout
Of lads that wore their honours out,
Runners whom renown outran
And the name died before the man.   20

So set, before its echoes fade,
The fleet foot on the sill of shade,
And hold to the low lintel up
The still-defended challenge-cup.

And round that early-laurelled head   25
Will flock to gaze the strengthless dead,
And find unwithered on its curls
The garland briefer than a girl's.

Notes:

You might like to look up the names Lillian Board and James Dean. Their stories
(though certainly not unique) are very appropriate to this poem.
Read "For the Fallen" (1914) by Laurence Binyon (1869-1943). It deals with
those young men who died in the first year of The Great War (1914-1918).

Read "Ode on a Grecian Urn" (1819) by John Keats (1795-1821). It also deals with a moment of intense experience frozen in time.

This poem is an elegy. Probably the most famous English poem in this genre is "Elegy Written in a Country Churchyard" (1750) by Thomas Gray (1716-1771). It is a bit long, but honestly it is worth the effort. Shorter, and more modern, is "Stop all the clocks" (1938) by W. H. Auden (1907-1973).

"The time you won your town the race" – Competitive races between towns and villages were a popular form of recreation in Victorian times.

"chaired you" – i.e., carried you seated on our shoulders.

"Shoulder-high we bring you home" – i.e., they are carrying his casket on their shoulders at his funeral.

"set you at your threshold down" – i.e., they lay down the coffin at the side of the grave, into which it will soon be lowered, thus passing, as through a doorway, into death.

"a stiller town" i.e., the graveyard (no exact location is specified) – an oxymoron.

"betimes" – i.e., before the expected time, early.

"the laurel" – i.e., the circle of laurel leaves placed on the head of a hero or champion.

"Cannot see the record cut" – i.e., he will not live to see his record for the course broken by someone else.

"rout" – i.e., a lawless assembly of people or a disorderly retreat of defeated troops (either way, the word has negative connotations).

"the sill of shade" – i.e., the edge of the grave. – metaphorically, the doorway of death.

"low lintel" – i.e., the horizontal support across the top of a door or window.

"still-defended challenge-cup" – Apparently the town still holds the cup that the runner won. Perhaps the young man died in the same year as his victory.

Guiding Questions:

1. What was the significance for the townspeople of the athlete's victory? Why did they celebrate it so extravagantly?

2. What similarities are there between the situations described in stanzas one and two? What are the essential differences?

3. What advantages does the speaker claim to find in the premature death of this superb athlete?

4. What inglorious fate does the speaker describe of those lads who achieved high "honours" in their youth but lived on into old age?

5. What is the setting of the final stanza? What is happening there?

6. Comment on the effectiveness of the poet's use of end-stopped and run-on lines.

Study Guide

Final thoughts:

Leggett finds this poem to be a fine example of the way in which the ostensible meaning of the speaker's words is undercut by the very words and rhythms he uses (or rather that Housman gives him) to express that meaning:

> The persona emphasizes in his graveside address the permanence achieved by the athlete, but the total effect of the poem is to reinforce a sense of transience, of the inescapable nature of change and death ... To equate his [the persona's] point of view with that of Housman is to confuse a technique by which the poet conveys a complex reaction to death with a philosophy, an abstract idea which has no meaning outside the poem. (*Poetic Art* 56-57)

Justly, this is one of the most famous and best-loved of A. E. Housman's poems. The title marks it as an elegy, that is, a poem composed on the occasion of someone's death. It is indeed a powerful eulogy for a young man who was once the human embodiment of physical fitness and prowess, but who died young, cut off in the full bloom of his youth. This is something with which readers can easily identify. The theme of the poem is another reason it is so impactful. Instead of presenting the death of a young man as a tragedy, the speaker argues that the athlete is better off to have died young. He's not saying that it is a cause for celebration, of course, but he is countering the natural despair that such a death would prompt.

The voice in the poem is that of someone who knew the dead man, who witnessed his triumph and took part in celebrating it. He is speaking at the actual moment of the man's burial, for he speaks not only to him but to those who are with him carrying the coffin to the grave-side. The speaker is older than the dead man whom he calls, "Smart lad," a term that only an older man would use. The burden of his message is the contrast between the mutability of life and the permanence that he sees the youth as having found in death.

Stanza two is an extended metaphor for death: life is a road which only leads to one place (our eternal "home"); we are all (whether we like it or not) runners on this road; and no matter how swiftly we run, each of us comes to the same end. (Compare *2 Timothy* 4.7: "I have fought the good fight, I have finished the race, I have kept the faith.") For readers, as for the athlete, youth is a time of physical vigor, during which fame and admiration can be achieved. The achievement and the popularity that youth wins us is, however, fleeting: as one's body ages, there will come younger men to better our, already forgotten, achievements. And then we die!

Two incidents are juxtaposed: having won a race for his town and set a new record time, being carried in triumph on the shoulders of the proud people of the town; and the same the townspeople again carrying him on their shoulders, though this time he is in a coffin. In stanza three, the speaker's wording grants the athlete a sense of agency. He is a, "Smart lad," for having slipped away because if he had lived on and grown old, he would have lived to see his glory fade and his record broken. He would have become one of those, "Runners whom renown outran," a line that encapsulates the fact that we are all subject to time. [Critics sometimes find in the poem hints that the young man committed suicide, but I do not find this in the poem. Remember that life was much more uncertain in the 1890s.]

Taken literally, the couplet, "And early though the laurel grows / It withers quicker than the rose" is inaccurate: the cut laurel far outlives the cut rose, which actually withers more quickly. As a countryman, Housman would have been perfectly aware of this; he is not speaking of real laurels and roses but metaphorically. The lines stress that human achievement (symbolized by the laurels) is even more fleeting that the bloom of a cut rose. There is nothing more pathetic, the speaker implies, than old men living on past glories that no one else cares about or remembers.

Stanza four offers a more realistic description of death that to some degree undercuts, or at least qualifies, the speaker's argument thus far. It opens with the poem's only example of personification, "Eyes the shady night has shut." Night, which is a symbol of death, has closed the young man's eyes forever: death here is active and the athlete passive – death takes from him all agency. Not only can he not see his record broken, he cannot see anything. The speaker's use of oxymoron in the line, "And silence sounds no worse than cheers," undercuts the ostensibly positive assertion because silence *cannot* sound of anything. One might also detect an element of oxymoron in the description of the graveyard as a "stiller town." A town is a place of hustle and bustle, of community and (well) life; the grave is not a town and it is not "stiller" – it is dead still. It seems then that the speaker over-reaches himself in his use of language in this stanza, which is a sure sign that the poet does not intend the reader to accept his argument uncritically.

The final stanza seems to draw on pagan visions of the afterlife (like the Viking Valhalla, where the brave warriors feast eternally and tell tales of their victories). Here the dead will flock around the runner and admire his garland of victory – a garland that on earth would have been "briefer than a girl's," but which will here remain "unwithered" for all eternity.

The poem is written in iambic tetrameter, four feet that follow an unstressed-stressed syllable pattern (e.g., "The **time** / you **won** / your **town** / the **race**"). The quatrains follow an A A B B rhyme scheme (i.e., rhyming couplets) throughout. The rhyme scheme gives the poem a kind of rhythmic feeling, almost like a nursery rhyme. On the metrical and rhyming regularity of the poem, the Shmoop editors comment:

> This sense of certainty in the form is especially interesting when
> we consider the *uncertainty* of the content. The athlete has died

unexpectedly. Life is fleeting and uncertain. We don't know how or when we will die. We don't know if we'll be remembered when we're gone. At least Housman gives us the comfort of A A B B. The form mirrors our desire for certainty in an uncertain world. (Shmoop Editorial Team. "To an Athlete Dying Young Form and Meter." *Shmoop*. Shmoop University, Inc., 11 Nov. 2008. Web. 15 Sep. 2019.)

This quotation brings us back to the point made by Leggett with which I began this commentary.

XX

Oh fair enough are sky and plain,
 But I know fairer far:
Those are as beautiful again
 That in the water are;

The pools and rivers wash so clean   5
 The trees and clouds and air,
The like on earth was never seen,
 And oh that I were there.

These are the thoughts I often think
 As I stand gazing down   10
In act upon the cressy brink
 To strip and dive and drown;

But in the golden-sanded brooks
 And azure meres I spy
A silly lad that longs and looks   15
 And wishes he were I.

Notes:

Whether intentionally or not, the poem recalls the suicide by drowning of that other victim of rejection by a lover, Ophelia. Read the description of her death by Queen Gertrude: "There is a willow grows aslant a brook..." (Shakespeare *Hamlet* Act 4 Scene 7).
"cressy" – Watercress is a rapidly growing, aquatic or semi-aquatic, plant.
"brink" – Both the edge of the pond and the edge of action (stripping off his clothes, diving in and drowning himself).
"azure meres" – i.e., bright blue (like a cloudless sky) small lakes.

Guiding Questions:

1. Explain the setting of the poem. Where is the speaker and what is he doing?
2. Why does he feel that the reflection of the natural world that he sees in "pools and rivers" is superior to the real thing?
3. What is he tempted to do when he has these thoughts?
4. What new thought strikes the speaker when he sees his own reflection in these same pools?

Final Thoughts:

This poem explores the truth of the aphorism (a concise statement that expresses an important truth) that 'The perfect is the enemy of the good.' The speaker regards the real world ("sky and plain") as only "fair enough." In contrast, the world he sees "in the water" seems to be washed "clean"; it has a purity "never seen" on earth. Symbolically this poses the choice between living in the real world or living in the world of the imagination (the world of poetry perhaps). No wonder he wishes he inhabited this better world. But, of course, the speaker is making a huge error: what he thinks is *in* the water is actually a reflection *on* the water – it doesn't actually exist!

In stanza three, it becomes clear that the speaker is critically examining these thoughts not experiencing them. He is able to put them in perspective: these are the thoughts he "often" has when he is tempted to drown himself. The word "often" indicates, of course, that he has never yet acted upon this impulse; he has simply come to the "brink" – the point at which he is *about* to "strip and dive and drown." The word "drown" is important here because it conveys the speaker's understanding that it is not possible to live in the "trees and clouds and air" under the water (as it is not possible to live wholly in the world of the imagination): the only choice is between living on in an imperfect world and committing suicide and not living in any world at all.

The final stanza makes clear that the speaker has chosen to live. The world of the water is still described in ways that make it sound perfect: the brooks are "golden-sanded," gold being the purest and most precious of metals, and the sky there is "azure." It is all, however, an illusion, as the lad trapped in the water (the speaker's own reflection) knows, because he "wishes he were I." Notice the force of the word "silly." Not only is it the first and only negative word used to describe the world-in-the-water, but it is far more negative than anything said to describe the (admittedly) imperfect world. By its use, the wish to escape into perfection is dismissed by the speaker as a childish delusion.

XXI   **BREDON HILL**

In summertime on Bredon
  The bells they sound so clear;
Round both the shires they ring them
  In steeples far and near,
  A happy noise to hear.   5

Here of a Sunday morning
  My love and I would lie
And see the coloured counties,
  And hear the larks so high
  About us in the sky.   10

The bells would ring to call her
  In valleys miles away:
"Come all to church, good people;
  Good people, come and pray."
  But here my love would stay.   15

And I would turn and answer
  Among the springing thyme,
"Oh, peal upon our wedding,
  And we will hear the chime,
  And come to church in time."   20

But when the snows at Christmas
  On Bredon top were strown,
My love rose up so early
  And stole out unbeknown
  And went to church alone.   25

They tolled the one bell only,
  Groom there was none to see,
The mourners followed after,
  And so to church went she,
  And would not wait for me.   30

The bells they sound on Bredon,
  And still the steeples hum.
"Come all to church, good people," –
  Oh, noisy bells, be dumb;
  I hear you, I will come.   35

Study Guide

Notes:

Read "The Going" (1912) by Thomas Hardy (1840-1928) which deals with the death of his first wife, Emma, from whom Hardy had been estranged for a number of years prior to her death in 1912.

"Bredon" – In a note, Housman tells us it is, "Pronounced Breedon." Bredon Hill is in Worcestershire, south-west of Evesham in the Vale of Evesham. At the summit, there are the remains of earthworks from an Iron Age hill fort (Kemerton Camp) abandoned in the 1st century A.D. after a considerable battle. There are also Roman earthworks and a number of ancient standing stones on the hill. At the summit is a small stone tower called 'Parsons Folly,' or simply 'the Tower.' It was built in the middle of the 18th Century as a summer house for John Parsons, the squire of Kemerton Court.

"both the shires" – i.e., Worcestershire and Gloucestershire.

"strown" – i.e., strewn.

"tolled the one bell only" – Compare "any man's death diminishes me, because I am involved in mankind, and therefore never send to know for whom the bell tolls; it tolls for thee" (John Donne [1572-1631] *Devotions Upon Emergent Occasions, Meditation XVII*). Note the use of the singular noun "bell."

Guiding Questions:

1. Why did the lad and his girl not obey the call of the Sunday church bells?
2. What promise did the lad make to those bells to placate them?
3. What happened at Christmas? Explain what is meant by the lines, "My love rose up so early / And stole out unbeknown / And went to church alone."
4. What final promise does the lad make to the bells?

Final Thoughts:

The first stanza sets the scene by describing the sound of the church bells in summer. The sounds do not originate on the hill itself (which has a tower but no church) but from all of the town and village churches "Round about." The speaker calls it, "A happy noise to hear." The word "happy" is consistent with the idyllic descriptions ("summertime ... so clear"), but the word "noise" is even more significant. It suggests that to the speaker the sound of the bells is *just* a noise (albeit a pleasant one); that is, it carries no religious or spiritual significance. [Housman, we know, was an atheist.]

The next three stanzas focus on a particular situation: on Sunday mornings in summer, he and his girlfriend would lie on Bredon Hill simply taking in the ravishing beauty of the scenery, "see the coloured counties / And hear the larks so high." One element of that beauty was the sound of the church bells. He writes, "The bells would ring to call her / In valleys miles away." The bells are personified; they are calling the people to morning service,

"'Come all to church, good people; / Good people come and pray.'" Importantly, however, the bells call only to "her," the girl the speaker loves, and not to him. This suggests that while he has lost his faith, she is still a believer – the bells threaten to separate the two even then. Nevertheless, despite of the calling of the bells and the church, his lover remained with him on the hill, "But here my love would stay." There is no evidence of a conflict within the girl: she happily chooses earthly over divine love. For his part, the lad responds to the church bells, speaking as directly to them as they have just spoken to the two lovers. Aware that he and his girl are ignoring the call of the bells, he promises that they will come to church when those same bells "peal upon our wedding [day]." Then, he says, they will both "come to church in time." The speaker means that they will come to church willingly, quickly, and so in good time for their wedding service. However, perceptive readers may see that the phrase is capable of a much darker interpretation.

Stanza five immediately changes the tone of the poem. Gone is the heat of summer, replaced by "snows at Christmas" strewn on the very grass where the lovers lay a few months before. This is a landscape of death and despair rather than joy, and we soon learn the reason. In almost a riddling way, he tells us, "My love rose up so early / And stole out unbeknown / And went to church alone." It is as though he cannot bring himself to state clearly that his girl died, suddenly and tragically young, and was buried in the churchyard. We learn that, on that day, in contrast to the Sundays in summer, only one bell sounded and it did not "ring" like the summer bells, it "tolled" – the former suggests vigor and joy, the latter solemnity and mourning. The other key difference from the summer is that this time the girl *did* heed the call of the bell to come to church and in doing so left her lover heartbroken and alone because she "would not wait for me." Did he attend the funeral? The poem does not say. Certainly, he was not there in the role of bridegroom, though he may have been there are one of the "mourners."

The final stanza completes the circle of the narration. The bells again "sound" on Bredon Hill, still calling believers to worship, and calling the speaker too, but he wants none of it. Where previously they made a "happy noise," now they seem to him to be "noisy" (which is very different) and he wishes them "dumb." The bells serve only to remind the speaker of the loss of his lover, an arbitrary death that has alienated him even more from God. The bells remain the same, of course; it is his life experiences that change the way he perceives them. Yet one thing he does know: eventually, like every person who has ever lived, he too will die and "come to church in time" for his burial. [Compare Hamlet speaking of death, "If it be not now, yet it will come" (*Hamlet* Act 5 Scene 2).] Cleanth Brooks draws attention to the "note of exasperation" in the final stanza, writing that "the irritated outburst against the noise of the bells – is a powerful, if indirect way, of voicing the speaker's sense of loss. All come to death; he will come to the churchyard too; but now that his sweetheart has been stolen from him, what does it matter *when* he comes" ("Alfred Edward Housman" in Ricks Ed. 73).

XXII

The street sounds to the soldiers' tread,
    And out we troop to see:
A single redcoat turns his head,
    He turns and looks at me.

My man, from sky to sky's so far,   5
    We never crossed before;
Such leagues apart the world's ends are,
    We're like to meet no more;

What thoughts at heart have you and I
    We cannot stop to tell;   10
But dead or living, drunk or dry,
    Soldier, I wish you well.

Notes

"A homosexual is not a man who loves homosexuals, but merely a man who, seeing a soldier, immediately wants to have him for a friend" (Marcel Proust, quoted in Graves 108-109).

"redcoat" – A red coat was the British infantryman's normal uniform in and out of combat from the 16th century to the start of the 20th century. Khaki Service Dress was introduced in 1902, but most infantry regiments, and some cavalry regiments, continued to wear scarlet on parade and off-duty.

Guiding Questions:

1. What is ironic about the speaker's use of the word "troop"? (Clue: think of the meanings of the word as a verb and as a noun.)
2. What thoughts go through the speaker's mind when he and the passing soldier exchange a glance?

Final Thoughts:

    The setting and the action are clear and simple, but the import of the action is tantalizingly ambiguous. A body of soldiers (a troop) is marching down a town or village street – the heavy alliteration of the 's' sound in lines one and two is the footfall of their marching feet. Perhaps they are going off to war or are simply moving to a different camp. Neither the reader nor the people who rush into the street to see them appear to know. Then one soldier turns his head to look directly at the speaker – the repetition of "turns," carried over the line-break, makes it clear that it is a deliberate action. Their eyes lock for a second or two, and then

93

the moment is gone. Yet in that moment, this anonymous soldier becomes, "My man," to the speaker. Notice how the plurals that open stanza one ("soldiers' ... we") have been replaced by singulars ("recoat ... his ... He ... me"): at that moment it is as though they are the only people in the street. If the speaker understands the significance of the soldier's glance, he does not say what it was. Could he have seen in it a sexual invitation or a warning? (We note that Oscar Wilde had been sentenced for gross indecency only the previous year.)

The remaining two stanzas switch to a different, though related, thought. For all the intimacy that the two shared in that one glance, the world is so vast that the speaker must concede that, just as they had never met before, so they will never meet again. Whatever each felt in that moment, they "cannot stop to tell." They are, to use an old cliché, ships that pass in the night. Yet the speaker is not untouched by what has happened. He wishes the soldier well, perhaps aware that soldiers live even more precarious lives than do civilians.

XXIII

The lads in their hundreds to Ludlow come in for the fair,
  There's men from the barn and the forge and the mill and the fold,
The lads for the girls and the lads for the liquor are there,
  And there with the rest are the lads that will never be old.

There's chaps from the town and the field and the till and the cart,   5
  And many to count are the stalwart, and many the brave,
And many the handsome of face and the handsome of heart,
  And few that will carry their looks or their truth to the grave.

I wish one could know them, I wish there were tokens to tell
  The fortunate fellows that now you can never discern;   10
And then one could talk with them friendly and wish them farewell
  And watch them depart on the way that they will not return.

But now you may stare as you like and there's nothing to scan;
  And brushing your elbow unguessed-at and not to be told
They carry back bright to the coiner the mintage of man,   15
  The lads that will die in their glory and never be old.

Notes:

Read "Men who March Away" (1914) by Thomas Hardy (1840-1928) which has the theme of young men going to war where many will die prematurely.
"stalwart" – i.e., loyal, reliable, and hardworking.
"nothing to scan" – i.e., no means of identifying them.
"the coiner" – i.e., God.

Guiding Questions:

1. How does the poet convey the vibrant life of the fair?
2. Explain what the speaker means when he says "there with the rest are the lads that will never be old."
3. Explain why there are few of the lads at the fair few "that will carry their looks or their truth to the grave." Where have you encountered this same thought earlier in the collection?
4. Why does the speaker wish that he could discern those who will die young? How would he act toward them?

Final Thoughts

   Housman wrote most of the poems two decades before the outbreak of the

First World War, and never served in the military (or showed any inclination to do so). If he is to be considered a war poet, then it must be as a poet of the Boer Wars (Dec 16, 1880 to Mar 23, 1881; and Oct 11, 1899 to May 31, 1902) in which his youngest brother was killed). This, however, is one of the poems that prompted Robert Lowell to write: "One feels that Housman foresaw the Somme."

The long lines of the first stanza are packed with detail. The speaker lists the young men who have come by origin and by their intention in coming (the conjunction "and" occurs four times in the first quatrain) and the result is a portrait of vibrant communal life. This is all changed in the last line when the speaker tells us that "there with the rest are the lads that will never be old." Here, enjoying the life of the fair, are the men who will die on some foreign field.

Stanza two returns to the tumbling listing of all of the chaps at the fair (the conjunction "and" occurs eight times in the second quatrain) and ends with a line that again deflates the energy the first three lines have generated, for amongst the crowds are "few that will carry their looks or their truth to the grave." Only those who die in battle will do so. In the next stanza he calls them the "fortunate fellows that now you can never discern" – a though we have encountered in "To an Athlete Dying Young." The speaker wishes that there was some way to know who these men are – some token that would identify them – so that he "could talk with them friendly and wish them farewell."

In the final stanza he expresses his regret that there is no way of identifying these men. Notice the metaphor: these men who will go back to their God as perfect as a freshly minted coin, not scratched and tarnished by their encounters with what Hamlet terms "The heart-ache and the thousand natural shocks / That flesh is heir to" (Shakespeare, *Hamlet* Act 3 Scene 1). They "will die in their glory and never be old."

Robert Lowell (above) may be right, but Housman's narrator is prevented from looking at the death of young men realistically; he insists on looking at it through the filter of his romantic vision of death in youth. As sad as were the deaths of those serving in the Empire, they were in scale as nothing compared to the wholesale slaughter on the Western Front between 1914 and 1918. In Housman's poem, those who die are the happy few; the battles of the First World War would wipe out a generation.

XXIV

Say, lad, have you things to do?
    Quick then, while your day's at prime.
Quick, and if 'tis work for two,
    Here am I, man: now's your time.

Send me now, and I shall go;   5
    Call me, I shall hear you call;
Use me ere they lay me low
    Where a man's no use at all;

Ere the wholesome flesh decay,
    And the willing nerve be numb,   10
And the lips lack breath to say,
    "No, my lad, I cannot come."

Notes:

"prime" – i.e., at its best., its greatest strength. There is an older meaning of "prime" now little used. In the Christian Church it refers to a service forming part of the Divine Office, traditionally said (or chanted) at the first hour of the day (i.e., 6 a.m.). Housman probably has both meanings in mind.

Guiding Questions:

1. What two reasons does the speaker give why the lad addressed should seize his moment and do whatever he wants to do now?

Final Thoughts:

The poem presents both the speaker and the person addressed as victims of the relentless forward movement of time. Each at present inhabits a tiny space in which they are at their "prime," but the speaker seems to know what the lad does not – that the moment will pass never to return. Notice the speaker's urgent use of the imperative voice ("Say ... Send me ... Call me ... Use me") and his repetition both of grammatical structures ("Send me ... Call me ... Use me") and of individual words ("Quick ... Quick ... now ... now ... I shall ... I shall ... Call ... call"). Thus, the first six lines of the poem are full of life and are a call to action.

This changes immediately on line seven. Now the poem uses alliteration to stress the opposite, the finality and lifelessness of death ("lay me low ... nerve be numb ... lips lack breath ... I cannot come"). These harsh, short sounds take all the energy from the rhythm of the lines.

XXV

This time of year a twelvemonth past,
    When Fred and I would meet,
We needs must jangle, till at last
    We fought and I was beat.

So then the summer fields about,   5
    Till rainy days began,
Rose Harland on her Sundays out
    Walked with the better man.

The better man she walks with still,
    Though now 'tis not with Fred: 10
A lad that lives and has his will
    Is worth a dozen dead.

Fred keeps the house all kinds of weather,
    And clay's the house he keeps;
When Rose and I walk out together   15
    Stock-still lies Fred and sleeps.

Notes:

Read the poem "'Out, Out—'" (1916) by Robert Frost (1874-1963) which also deals with the way people react to a sudden death. The final two lines are particularly appropriate, "No more to build on there. And they, since they / Were not the one dead, turned to their affairs." Are the people right or wrong to turn away from the dead and get on with their own living?

"jangle" – Literally a discordant metallic sound. Here it means that they argued a lot. Compare Ophelia's description of what she takes to be insanity in Hamlet, "Now see that noble and most sovereign reason / Like sweet bells jangled, out of tune and harsh" (Shakespeare *Hamlet* Act 3 Scene 1).

"on her Sundays out" – This suggests that Rose was in service, perhaps as a maid in a local house.

"keeps the house" – i.e., stays inside the house.

Guiding Questions:

1. In what sense did Fred prove himself a "better man" than the speaker?
2. In what sense did the speaker prove himself a "better man" than Fred?

Final Thoughts:

The ironies of this poem revolve around the phrase "the better man." The speaker and another young man were rivals for the affection of Rose Harland, and settled their rivalry: Fred proved himself the better man by beating the speaker in a fist fight. (I think we can acquit Rose of any hand in this; probably she did not even know about it.) However, Fred died a few months later and now the speaker is the better men because he is alive and with the dead man's girl. (Again, I do not think that the poem wants us to be too hard on Rose: her boyfriend died and, presumably after a period of grief, she began walking out with another man. What else is she expected to do?) The moral of the poem is short and cynical, "A lad that lives and has his will / Is worth a dozen dead." Notice the paired alliteration at the beginning and end of this clause ("A **l**ad that **l**ives … a **d**ozen **d**ead"). The rising emphasis of the 'l' alliteration contrasts with the hard finality of the 'd' alliteration.

The point of the poem is not the character of the participants but their helplessness in the face of fate. The young man who has everything (is handsome, has got the girl) suddenly is nothing – literally. The living Fred "would meet … jangle … fought … walked." These emphatic verbs in the first two stanzas convey his agency. However, in the last two stanzas, only the speaker has agency (he "walks … has his will … walk[s] out together"). In contrast, Fred is defined by his stasis (he "keeps the house … Stock still lies … sleeps"). The short vowels and 's' alliteration stress the finality of Fred's fate, "Stock-still lies Fred and sleeps."

The speaker includes some play on words that is almost cruel. Fred, who used to walk out with Rose in the sunshine now "keeps the house all kinds of weather" – a total reversal. As though the reader has not solved the riddle of the house in this line, he tells us, "clay's the house he keeps" (i.e., his grave). The phrase is a typical oxymoron describing death, which is nothing at all like life, in terms of life. (Compare "a stiller town" in "To an Athlete Dying Young.")

XXVI

    Along the fields as we came by
A year ago, my love and I,
The aspen over stile and stone
Was talking to itself alone.
"Oh who are these that kiss and pass?   5
A country lover and his lass;
Two lovers looking to be wed;
And time shall put them both to bed,
But she shall lie with earth above,
And he beside another love."   10

    And sure enough beneath the tree
There walks another love with me,
And overhead the aspen heaves
Its rainy-sounding silver leaves;
And I spell nothing in their stir,   15
But now perhaps they speak to her,
And plain for her to understand
They talk about a time at hand
When I shall sleep with clover clad,
And she beside another lad.   20

Notes:

"aspen" – "Aspen trees are all native to cold regions with cool summers, in the north of the Northern Hemisphere, extending south at high-altitude areas such as mountains or high plains. They are all medium-sized deciduous trees reaching 15–30 m (49–98 ft) tall. In North America, it is referred to as Quaking Aspen or Trembling Aspen because the leaves 'quake' or tremble in the wind." (Wikipedia contributors. "Aspen." *Wikipedia, The Free Encyclopedia*. Wikipedia, The Free Encyclopedia, 14 Jul. 2019. Web. 21 Sep. 2019.)

"stile and stone" – A stile is an arrangement of steps or a narrow gap that allows people but not animals to climb over or walk through a fence or wall. Presumably the field boundaries are drystone wall.

"her" – In line sixteen "her" refers to the second young lady whom the speaker has begun courting following the death of the first.

Guiding Questions:

1. What, one year ago, did the aspen trees know about the fate of the two lovers?
2. What does it now know of the fate of the speaker and the girl with whom he is walking out?

Final Thoughts:

Once again, the theme of this poem is the contrast between the mortality of people and the (apparent) immortality of nature. There is something pagan (perhaps Druidic) about attributing mystical powers of divination to the trees. A year ago, the aspen trees knew that the "country lover and his lass" would never wed because the young woman would die and he would take up with another girl. Only in hindsight does the speaker claim to understand that this is what the aspens were saying.

In stanza two, he is walking with this new love and once again he hears the sound of the wind through the leaves. He tells us that for him they have no meaning, "I spell nothing in their stir," but wonders if they are speaking to his new girl and telling her that he will die and she will walk "beside another lad." The finality of death is conveyed by short, sharp 's' and 'c' alliteration, "I shall sleep with clover clad." The poem really evokes a sense of the despair of lost love in the face of death.

The poem is written in rhyming couplets, the rhyming words being (with three exceptions) monosyllables and full rhymes. Not one of the rhymes appears forced; the reader hardly notices how perfectly they give structure to the verse. The lines are written in regular iambic tetrameter (four iambs per line, e.g., "**Along** the **fields** as **we** came **by**"). Housman's use of traditional verse forms and simple language is shown at its best.

XXVII

"Is my team ploughing,
    That I was used to drive
And hear the harness jingle
    When I was man alive?"

Ay, the horses trample,   5
    The harness jingles now;
No change though you lie under
    The land you used to plough.

"Is football playing
    Along the river shore,   10
With lads to chase the leather,
    Now I stand up no more?"

Ay, the ball is flying,
    The lads play heart and soul;
The goal stands up, the keeper   15
    Stands up to keep the goal.

"Is my girl happy,
    That I thought hard to leave,
And has she tired of weeping
    As she lies down at eve?"   20

Ay, she lies down lightly,
    She lies not down to weep:
Your girl is well contented.
    Be still, my lad, and sleep.

"Is my friend hearty,   25
    Now I am thin and pine,
And has he found to sleep in
    A better bed than mine?"

Yes, lad, I lie easy,
    I lie as lads would choose;   30
I cheer a dead man's sweetheart,
    Never ask me whose.

Notes

Read "Ah, Are You Digging on My Grave?" (1913) by Thomas Hardy (1840-1928). It is a satirical dialogue that exposes romantic or sentimental illusions about love, life, and death.

"to chase the leather" – i.e., to run after the soccer ball.

Guiding Questions:

1. Explain why four of the stanzas are enclosed by speech marks and four are not.
2. The dead man mentions four activities/concerns he had when he was living. Do you notice a progression in these?
3. What is the point of the dead man's questions? What answers is he looking for?
4. What answers does he get?
5. How do you react to finding out that the dead man's best friend is now sleeping with his girl? (Given the era in which this was written, we can assume they are married.)

Final Thoughts:

The poem employs the simple style of traditional folk ballads, featuring a question-and-answer format. It has eight stanzas each one of which is a quatrain with a rhyme scheme of A B C B. The dialogue is between a dead man, whose words are differentiated by being placed in speech marks, and his still-living friend. The former is enquiring whether the life he knew when he was alive still goes on. This suggests that the man's spirit is restless; he is still looking backward on his life, perhaps hoping that he is remembered and that his death has made a significant difference. The friend's answer is in the affirmative, but with one important qualification: life does go on, but is now others live it, others fulfil the roles of those who have died. Everything goes on as it did before the poor dead farmer's body was placed "under / The land [he] used to plough." Our deaths do not cause permanent disturbance in everyone's lives: people adapt – as they must. Man is mortal but community is permanent.

The contrast throughout is between the activity of the living (like the lads who "play heart and soul" at soccer) and the inactivity of the dead man. While he lies motionless in his grave and will "stand up no more," the goal "stands up, the keeper / Stands up to keep the goal"; and his girlfriend "lies not down to weep," but to make love with his best friend, and that friend "lie[s] easy, / I lie as lads would choose." The dead man alone has been robbed of choice and agency. The friend's purpose is to reconcile the dead man's spirit to the realities of life and death, "Be still, my lad, and sleep," and to protect him about the troubling truth of mortal transience.

The progression of the dead man's questions is from the impersonal to the personal: his work, his play and finally his love. There is similarly a progression in the answers of his friend: from the indirect to the direct. First, he confirms that "the horses trample, / The harness jingles now." This implies, without actually stating, that someone else drives the dead man's horse plough. Second, he confirms, "The goal stands up, the keeper / Stands up to keep the goal." What is unsaid (but implied) is that the dead man used to play in that position (see also XVII) and now someone else has his place. Third, he confirms that the dead man's girl "lies not down to weep" and "is well contented," but without giving any reason. Forth, and finally, he confirms that he himself lies "easy." Only then does he reveal the reason, "I cheer a dead man's sweetheart, / Never ask me whose." The caution in the final line is redundant – the dead man has finally heard the truth: someone guides his plough; someone plays in his soccer position; his girl no longer weeps for him; and his best friend sleeps with her.

Thus, the poem presents an ironic contrast between the transience of an individual man and the enduring cycle of mankind. The speaker's questions reveal his naivety: he regards certain elements of his life (and most importantly his love of his girl) as permanent and unchanging. He assumes that his sweetheart can only have achieved happiness if she has "tired of weeping," as if only mourning could purge her grief. It simply has not occurred to him that she might have turned to another man for comfort. As gently as he can, his friend shatters the dead youth's conviction of the permanence of love.

How are we to judge the actions of those who turn to their own affairs since they are not the one dead? Is the friend really a friend who wants the dead man's spirit to find peace, or is he a disloyal traitor? The poem raises questions that it does not answer.

XXVIII   *THE WELSH MARCHES*

High the vanes of Shrewsbury gleam
Islanded in Severn stream;
The bridges from the steepled crest
Cross the water east and west.

The flag of morn in conqueror's state   5
Enters at the English gate:
The vanquished eve, as night prevails,
Bleeds upon the road to Wales.

Ages since the vanquished bled
Round my mother's marriage-bed;   10
There the ravens feasted far
About the open house of war:

When Severn down to Buildwas ran
Coloured with the death of man,
Couched upon her brother's grave   15
The Saxon got me on the slave.

The sound of fight is silent long
That began the ancient wrong;
Long the voice of tears is still
That wept of old the endless ill.   20

In my heart it has not died,
The war that sleeps on Severn side;
They cease not fighting, east and west,
On the marches of my breast.

Here the truceless armies yet   25
Trample, rolled in blood and sweat;
They kill and kill and never die;
And I think that each is I.

None will part us, none undo
The knot that makes one flesh of two,   30
Sick with hatred, sick with pain,
Strangling – When shall we be slain?

When shall I be dead and rid
Of the wrong my father did?
How long, how long, till spade and hearse   35
Put to sleep my mother's curse?

Notes:

A similar theme of mixed inheritance is explored in the novel *Sons and Lovers* (1913) by D. H. Lawrence (1885-1930). The protagonist, Paul Morel, is the product of a union between a prim and proper middle-class mother and a vibrant, erratic working-class miner.

"Welsh Marches" – The term dates back to the Middle Ages to describe the disputed border area between Western England and Eastern Wales. Edward I, King of England, annexed Wales under the Statute of Wales in 1284, but not until 1536 did the Act of Union, declared by King Henry VIII, incorporate Wales within his realm. For centuries this was land constantly fought over. Through the centuries, and particularly following the unification of England and Wales, there was considerable mixing of the two cultures through intermarriage. English inevitably became the dominant culture and efforts were made to eradicate native Welsh culture.

"vanes" – A weather vane (wind vane or weathercock) is an instrument used for showing the direction of the wind. They are often located on the tops of buildings – in this case church steeples. The skyline of Shrewsbury is dominated by the steeples of its many ancient churches.

"Shrewsbury" – The old part of the county town of Shropshire was built within a meander (i.e., a wide loop) of the River Severn since this made it easier to defend.

"steepled crest" – On the highest hill in Shrewsbury stands St. Alkmund's Church which has the third highest spire of any parish church in England. It is 68 meters tall.

"The bridges ... / Cross the water east and west" – Because the loop of the Severn is almost a full circle, there are bridges on both the (English) east side of the town and the (Welsh) west side.

"flag of morn" – i.e., the sun.

"Bleeds upon" – A reference to the red of the sunset.

"ravens" – Ravens are black, noisy and aggressive. In winter, especially, ravens are scavengers and feed on carrion.

"Buildwas" – This village, just under twelve miles south east of Shrewsbury, was mentioned in *Domesday Book* (1086). It is the site of a Cistercian Abbey founded in 1135.

"Coloured with the death of man" – i.e., literally running red with the blood of those killed in battle.

"The Saxon got me on the slave" – The post-Roman inhabitants of the British

Isles, the Celtic Britons, were gradually pushed further to the west after the arrival of the Anglo-Saxons in the 5th century. The last stronghold of the Britons was what is known today as Wales. The subjugation of the Welsh and their culture did not end until the mid-twentieth century. As with the attempts in the USA to 'educate' Native Americans out of their culture, so school students were flogged in Wales for speaking their own language, English being the sole language of instruction. Since the mid-twentieth century there has been a concerted effort to preserve and value the Welsh language and culture.

Guiding Questions:

1. What impression do you get of the town of Shrewsbury from the description in stanza one?
2. In stanza two the sunrise and sunset are described in very metaphorical terms. With what is each compared? Why?
3. What act do stanzas three and four describe? How is that act connected to the speaker? (Or, if you prefer, how does the speaker *feel* that the action is connected with himself?)
4. Stanzas five, six and seven describe the speaker's own psychology. Explain the conflict that goes on endlessly in his head and heart.
5. What does the speaker see as the only solution for the divided consciousness from which he suffers?

Final Thoughts:

This poem is a good illustration of the need to differentiate the persona who speaks in a poem from the artist who wrote the poem. "The Welsh Marches" shows a psyche riven (i.e., a man being pulled in two directions psychologically) by the speaker's dual Anglo-Welsh heritage, forever at war within himself, even though the bloody border battles are long passed. Housman was not from Shropshire, he was born in Worcester. His father was from Lancaster, his mother from Worcester (though she had a Welsh name, Williams), and they were married in Gloucester. In contrast, speaker in the poem is a descendent (generations back in time) of a Welsh mother and an English father and feels this division within himself.

The opening stanza gives no indication of the conflict to follow. It provides an aerial view of the town of Shrewsbury which emphasizes the weather vanes on the many steeples, the peaceful security of the town almost enclosed by the river, and the bridges which connect it with both England and Wales. It is an idyllic picture: the weather vanes "gleam," the town is "Islanded" (i.e., protected) by the river, and bridges link the town with "east and west." Everything seems to be perfect.

In stanza two the speaker describes sunrise and sunset – appropriate matter, one would think, for a continuation of the idyll. The description, however, makes use of imagery that evokes the violent past on the Anglo-Welsh border. The rising sun is described as the "flag of morn" that comes "in conqueror's state" through the "English gate," metaphorically recalling the rising, overpowering military power of the English, which like the morning sun, rose in the east. In this context, the reader may suspect a play on words in the phrase the "flag of morn," which contains a homonym for 'mourn,' recalling the sufferings and anguish of the Welsh at the hands of the English. At sunset, the gathering darkness of "night prevails," spreading from the east and thus symbolizing the victorious English. Meanwhile, the "vanquished eve" metaphorically represents the Britons/Welsh in retreat, their blood strewn along "the road to Wales."

Stanza three is referring to an ancient battle (although not, perhaps, to a specific historical battle). It has been "Ages" since the vanquished Britons lay bleeding and the "ravens feasted far / About the open house of war." The ravens were freely feeding on the dead slain in the battle. He says that the dead and dying lay "Round my mother's marriage-bed." What he means by this metaphor, will only become clear in the next stanza.

Stanza four describes a horrific rape which happened after the battle he has described. When the Severn ran red with blood downstream from Shrewsbury to the village of Buildwas, then his ancestral mother, a Welsh Briton, was raped by one of the victorious Saxons, "Couched upon her brother's grave," on the site where her dead brother lay, in the middle of the battlefield. Now we recognize that the reference to his ancestral mother's "marriage-bed" in the previous stanza was bitterly ironic: what happened was not a marriage; it was not consensual, "The Saxon got me on the slave." The use of the phrase "got me" stresses the absence of tenderness; the Saxon was simply enjoying a right of conquest. While in stanza two the contrast is between "conqueror" and "vanquished," here it is between "Saxon" and "slave."

Stanza five returns to the present, centuries after the battle. The words "ancient" and "old," together with the repetition of the word "long," stress that the sounds of warfare (both of the fighting and the weeping) have been silent for centuries. The aggression of the Saxons against Welsh is an "ancient wrong," but yet the speaker calls it "the endless ill," intimating that although the physical fighting is in the past, the injustice and its resulting psychological damage (a sort of ancestral PTSD) is still current.

In stanza six, the speaker tells us that the war "sleeps on Severn side." The alliteration of the long 's' sound together with the long, slow 'e' vowels conveys a peaceful sense. But, he adds, it is in his own heart and mind that the struggle of Briton against Saxon continues, "On the marches of my breast." Here the alliteration of the harsh 'm' sound, together with the clipped vowel sounds set a different tone. Within himself, "They cease not fighting, east and west." In the next stanza, the speaker describes how he still feels the dissension and division within himself. The disjoined rhythm of the lines begins with the run-on between lines 25 and 26, and in the harsh, short alliteration of the 't' sound ("**t**ruceless armies yet / **T**rample..."). It continues in the repetition of the staccato monosyllables "kill and kill," and in the cumulative impact of three 'ands.' The result is a turmoil of language that mirrors the turmoil within the speaker which comes from the fact that, in this endless inner conflict between his Welsh and Saxon ancestry "each is I" – that is, being Anglo-Welsh, he identifies with both sides.

The speaker feels himself to be caught in a "knot that makes one flesh of two." This metaphor likens the binding of two ropes into one with the that biological parentage that binds his Saxon/English and Briton/Welsh selves. Paradoxically, they are "one flesh" but they are not one heart and mind, and he suffers psychologically from the internal struggle, "sick with hatred, sick with pain." The effect is "Strangling," constricting. Notice the power that the word is given by being isolated at the start of the line. He has no clear sense of who he is, but feels himself split into two selves each of which hates the other. He asks rhetorically, "When shall we be slain?" for the only salvation he sees is death.

In the final stanza, the speaker continues to wonder when death will end his internal struggle. In his tortured state, he believes that only death will "rid [him] / Of the wrong my father did," specifically the rape of his ancestral mother by a victorious Saxon, and more generally the destruction by the Anglo-Saxons of the more ancient British/Welsh culture. The reader senses his despair in the repetition of the phrase, "How long, how long." Only the "spade and hearse," he feels can, "Put to sleep my mother's curse." By this he means the pain he has inherited from his Welsh side – the pain felt by the defeated and the raped.

This is one of Housman's most complex and satisfying poems in which he seems to escape the restriction of his own feelings to tap into a more universal theme.

XXIX THE LENT LILY

'Ts spring; come out to ramble
The hilly brakes around,
For under thorn and bramble
About the hollow ground
The primroses are found.   5

And there's the windflower chilly
With all the winds at play,
And there's the Lenten lily
That has not long to stay
And dies on Easter day.   10

And since till girls go maying
You find the primrose still,
And find the windflower playing
With every wind at will,
But not the daffodil,   20

Bring baskets now, and sally
Upon the spring's array,
And bear from hill and valley
The daffodil away
That dies on Easter day.   25

Notes:

Read "I wandered lonely as a cloud" (1804-1807) by William Wordsworth (1770-1850). It is certainly the most famous poem about encountering daffodils – at least in English.

Read "To the Virgins, to Make Much of Time" (1648) by Robert Herrick (1591-1674) which uses roses to make much the same point as Housman makes by referencing daffodils. It begins:

> Gather ye rosebuds while ye may,
> Old Time is still a-flying…

"The Lent Lily" – i.e., the daffodil. Lent begins on Ash Wednesday and ends approximately six weeks later on the Saturday before Easter Sunday. Some Christians fast and/or give up certain luxuries to replicate the sacrifice of Jesus Christ who spent forty days in the desert wilderness.

"hilly brakes" – i.e., "rough or marshy land overgrown usually with one kind of plant" (Merriam-Webster).

"maying" – i.e., celebrating May Day (May 1st) by dancing and gathering spring flowers.

"array" – i.e., impressive display.

Guiding Questions:

1. Make a list of the springtime vegetation mentioned in the poem. Explain what is unique about the daffodil that makes it stand out from all of the others.
2. What action does the speaker call for?

Final Thoughts:

Spring is the season of rebirth in the world of flora and of generation in the world of fauna. For humans it is associated with love: "In spring a young man's fancy lightly turns to thoughts of love" (Alfred Tennyson). In this poem the speaker calls on his lover to come out and "ramble" around the countryside. "The hilly brakes" with their "thorn and bramble" do not sound very appealing, but the speaker knows that one has only to look carefully to find primroses, wildflowers and daffodils. This is a metaphor for life itself: man's time on earth may be short and often bitter, but there are compensating beauties if only we take the trouble to find them. While primroses and wildflowers bloom for a long time, the daffodil traditionally (though not in fact), "dies on Easter day." In early May, "You find the primrose still [flowering]." Unlike the longer-stemmed wildflowers, primroses are also "still" because they grow close to the ground and are less affected by the wind. In contrast, you "find the windflower playing / With every wind at will." The daffodils, however, are long gone. Rather than see this as a reason for despair, the speaker presents it as a reason for taking as much pleasure as possible in the passing beauty of the daffodils – gather your daffodils while you may!

The religious implications of the poem are impossible to avoid. For believing Christians, Easter is not about the death of Christ but his resurrection and the hope of eternal life that it brings. There is no reference to resurrection in the poem. For the speaker, Easter illustrates, in the fate of the daffodil, the brevity of all life. The consolation that Christians gain from the message of the Cross is absent. Rather the message is to enjoy beauty while it is available. The speaker urges his lover to "Bring baskets" to hold the daffodils they will gather. He urges her to "sally / Upon the spring's array." The aggressive way he intends to capture the beauty of the daffodils is conveyed in the use of the military term "sally" which means to make a sudden charge out of a besieged place (winter?) against the enemy. The military metaphor continues when he says they will "bear from hill and valley / The daffodil away," which refers to soldiers looting and carrying away treasures from a conquered town. Evidently, this poem takes a more positive view of life than many others in the collection.

XXX

Others, I am not the first,
Have willed more mischief than they durst:
If in the breathless night I too
Shiver now, 'tis nothing new.

More than I, if truth were told,   5
Have stood and sweated hot and cold,
And through their reins in ice and fire
Fear contended with desire.

Agued once like me were they,
But I like them shall win my way   10
Lastly to the bed of mould
Where there's neither heat nor cold.

But from my grave across my brow
Plays no wind of healing now,
And fire and ice within me fight   15
Beneath the suffocating night.

Notes:

"Agued" – i.e., fevered.
"bed of mould" – i.e., the grave.

Guiding Questions:

1. This is a poem largely without a setting. Where do you imagine the speaker to be and what do you imagine him to be doing – or to be contemplating doing?
2. Do you think he will do it? Explain your answer.

Final Thoughts:

I imagine the speaker on the street before a house. It is night, and he is planning to break into the house and steal whatever of value he can find. He is only waiting to summon up the courage to begin. He cannot yet quite bring himself to do it.

Of course, none of this is in the poem. There is no indication of the setting and no description of the man's actions. That, I take it, is the whole point. The poem is not about a particular temptation; it is about temptation in general. The man has "sweated hot and cold" like a man in a fever, caught between hot desire and cold fear, "fire and ice within me fight." This is really a companion piece to the last poem: since life is short, grab what you can when you can. The only difference is that collecting daffodils is not illegal but stealing is. Thus, there is an added dimension to this poem. If there is no God, then there are no transcendent moral values. As Dostoyevsky warned, "If God is dead, then everything is permitted."

Leggett writes:

> [The persona] is presented as a young man dealing with his first taste of the desire and guilt which are the fruits of experience ... The theme of private versus shared experience achieves a curious effect in the poem, for the speaker's determination to console himself with the knowledge that his feelings have been shared by other men serves only to reinforce the sense of their privacy ... The persona's response to his situation is obviously inadequate, as he casts about for ways to find release from his strong feelings ... The poem reveals the inadequacy of the intellect, the domination of the feelings... (*Poetic Art* 51).

XXXI

On Wenlock Edge the wood's in trouble;
   His forest fleece the Wrekin heaves;
The gale, it plies the saplings double,
   And thick on Severn snow the leaves.

'Twould blow like this through holt and hanger   5
   When Uricon the city stood:
'Tis the old wind in the old anger,
   But then it threshed another wood.

Then, 'twas before my time, the Roman
   At yonder heaving hill would stare: 10
The blood that warms an English yeoman,
   The thoughts that hurt him, they were there.

There, like the wind through woods in riot,
   Through him the gale of life blew high;
The tree of man was never quiet: 15
   Then 'twas the Roman, now 'tis I.

The gale, it plies the saplings double,
   It blows so hard, 'twill soon be gone:
To-day the Roman and his trouble
   Are ashes under Uricon.   20

Notes:

"Wenlock Edge" – Wenlock Edge in Shropshire is a wooded limestone escarpment, approximately 1,083 feet above sea level, that runs for almost twenty miles southwest to northeast between Craven Arms and Much Wenlock. It affords stunning views.
"Wrekin" – The Wrekin in Shropshire is a wooded hill, 1,335 feet above sea level, situated five miles to the north of Wenlock Edge. On the summit is an Iron Age Hill Fort. The Severn River winds between the two uplands.
"plies" – i.e., bends., doubles over.
"saplings" – i.e., young trees.
"holt" – i.e., a small wood, a copse. An archaic, Anglo-Saxon word.
"hanger" – i.e., a wood on the side of a steep hill. Another archaic, Anglo-Saxon word.
"Uricon" – There was a large Roman settlement near Shrewsbury at Wroxeter called Viroconium or Uriconium.

"threshed" – An agricultural term used to describe beating ripe grain from harvested stalks of wheat or barley.

"the Roman" – The Romans controlled Britain (or at least significant parts of it) from 43 to 410 AD.

Guiding Questions:

1. What is troubling the woods on Wenlock Edge and Wrekin Hill?
2. Explain why the wind is the same wind as in Roman times but the trees are different.
3. The speaker feels a deep empathy for the Roman who might have stood on the same spot he is standing on. Explain why.
4. Why will, "The gale ... soon be gone"?
5. The Roman is long dead and the speaker will soon be dead. Is there any glimmer of positivity in the poem's conclusion?

Final Thoughts:

An anonymous analysis of this poem on the *Interesting Literature* Blog calls it "one of the greatest poetic meditations on the smallness of the individual life when set against the grand sweep of history." That seems right to me.

The first stanza introduces the theme of agitation: the wood on Wenlock Edge is "in trouble," disturbed by high winds. Five miles away, the trees that cover the Wrekin as thickly as fleece covers the back of a sheep likewise heave in the wind. Notice the personification of the woods in each case: to feel troubled by the wind and to heave (i.e., rise and fall, pant), the woods must have human qualities. So destructive is the storm that "thick on Severn snow the leaves." The metaphor of snow suggests cold and even death.

Stanza two takes us back almost two millennia. Then winds exactly like those at present would blow "through holt and hanger." Housman carefully selects two words whose origin goes back at least to Anglo-Saxon times. Then the speaker makes an important distinction: the wind is the same (it is "the old wind in the old anger"), but the woods are different – these are not the same trees that grew here, "When Uricon the city stood." This leads in the next stanza to the thought that, similarly, the individual men (like the individual trees) have changed: then it was a Roman and now it is "an English yeoman." Nevertheless, their basic humanity is the same. The thoughts and feelings that "hurt" the Victorian speaker were also present in the mind and heart of the Roman, "they were there." Thus, the poem provides an ironic contrast between the historical perspective, symbolized by the ruins on the hill, and the timeless perspective represented by the wind imagery – the former lineal and the latter cyclical.

Stanza four states that the Roman and the Victorian men share the experience of being buffeted by the storms of experience which the speaker calls, "the gale of life." What is constant is not individual men, who obviously come and go, but, "The tree of man," which symbolizes the inevitably troubled state of being human. That tree is "never quiet"; indeed, the winds of trouble blow so fiercely that they "double" not only the saplings but the men. Yet the final stanza introduces an entirely new idea: the storm of life "blows so hard, 'twill soon be gone." He does not mean that the period of trouble will pass as quickly as a bad storm passes on the hills of Wenlock and Wrekin giving way to a period of calm and tranquility that the human can enjoy in peace; he means rather that the storms will soon be gone because you die. The Roman is long gone; both he and his troubles, "Are ashes under Uricon." Similarly, the speaker recognizes that both he and his troubles will soon be ashes as well. This suggests a stoical rather than a pessimistic perspective.

At first reading, the conclusion of the poem is purely bleak. The American rapper Nas (Nasir bin Olu Dara Jones) writes, "Life's a bitch and then you die." The solution in the Nas lyric is to "get high," but I think that Housman, or at least his speaker, hints at another perspective. Life in this poem is, indeed, presented as endless trouble, but it is also presented as brief. To say the least, this puts our sense of trouble into perspective: life may be, in the words of philosopher Thomas Hobbes (1588-1679) "solitary, poor, nasty, brutish and short" (*Leviathan* 1651)*, but it is all we have and as such it has value. "On Wenlock Edge" is written in iambic tetrameter, with each stanza rhymed A B A B, a common quatrain form and rhyme scheme in Housman.

* To be fair to Thomas Hobbes, he was talking about human life in the pre-societal, natural state.

XXXII

From far, from eve and morning
  And yon twelve-winded sky,
The stuff of life to knit me
  Blew hither: here am I.

Now – for a breath I tarry   5
  Nor yet disperse apart –
Take my hand quick and tell me,
  What have you in your heart.

Speak now, and I will answer;
  How shall I help you, say;   10
Ere to the wind's twelve quarters
  I take my endless way.

Notes:

Go to YouTube and search for the song "Pastures of Plenty" by Woody Guthrie. You will find several versions. The song contains the line, "We come with the dust and we go with the wind," which is reminiscent of Housman's poem – though Guthrie's lyrics are more about political activism.

The first stanza – Mr. Emerson quotes this stanza in *A Room with a View* (1908) by E. M. Forster (1879-1970), Chapter II: "In Santa Croce with No Baedeker." Mr. Emerson comments, "'George [Mr. Emerson's son] and I both know this, but why does it distress him? We know that we come from the winds, and that we shall return to them; that all life is perhaps a knot, a tangle, a blemish in the eternal smoothness. But why should this make us unhappy?'Let us rather love one another, and work and rejoice.'" Here Forster (very much a Housman fan) sums up the poet's position in *A Shropshire Lad*. George's problem is that life in an entirely random universe appears to be meaningless. Until, that is, he falls in love with Lucy Honeychurch after which his existence has meaning.

"twelve-winded sky" – Ancient diagrams of the compass typically indicated twelve winds.

"The stuff of life to knit me" – The King James Version translates *Psalms* 139.13: "For thou hast possessed my reins: thou hast covered me in my mother's womb." However, other translations use the phrase "knit me" as in The English Standard version: "For you formed my inward parts; you knitted me together in my mother's womb."

"endless way" – Housman uses similar phrases "ceaseless way" (XXXVI) and "endless road" (LX).

Study Guide

Guiding Questions:

1. What alternative to the creation myth of Adam and Eve is presented in the first stanza? How is the creation myth presented here different from that in *Genesis*?
2. How will the component parts that make up the speaker "disperse apart"? What do you notice about that phrase?
3. About what should the speaker's companion, "Speak now."

Final Thoughts:

In stanza one, the speaker reflects that the "stuff of life" – literally the elements and molecules that compose his body and his mind – came together quite by chance. The components of life, "Blew hither" and "knit" together to form each living being in a completely random way. The wind to which he refers which gathered the constituents of life, "From far, from eve and morning," is not an earthly but a cosmic wind from "yon twelve-winded sky." Today, we might now say that the universe was created by a 'Big Bang' and that matter coalesced to form stars, on at least one of which the elements necessary for life happened to come together. Out of the most basic amoeba, complex life forms evolved capable of movement and reproduction, and in humans, consciousness of identity, of learning and of emotions. All this happened by chance. "Here am I," the speaker asserts.

Stanza two explores the nature of this life that the speaker experiences. As Gale Rhodes writes, "In the grand scheme of the universe, each of us is here for only a moment" ("A Metaphor for Evolution"). The speaker is aware that his constituent parts will only hold together "for a breath" before they "disperse apart." The word "breath" relates back to the idea of cosmic wind, but how much smaller it is! Technically, the phrase "disperse apart" is a tautology (i.e., it says the same thing twice in different words). This is done for emphasis.

On line seven, the speaker suddenly addresses another person, a companion. Given the brevity of life, he says, there is no time for delay, "Take my hand quick and tell me, / What have you in your heart"; there is no time to lose in hesitation, circumlocution or euphemism. He urges his friend, "Speak now, and I will answer; / How shall I help you, say." The realization that life is only a passing moment in eternity serves to impress upon the speaker the need to experience that moment to its fullest intensity. Interestingly, there is not even a hint of anything sexual here (though honesty about one's affections and sexual needs would obviously be included in the speaker's statement about the need for total honesty between people). We have only a brief window before our constituent molecules fall apart again and disperse into the universe. This being so, we must take every opportunity to relate to and to support another human being.

XXXIII

If truth in hearts that perish
   Could move the powers on high,
I think the love I bear you
   Should make you not to die.

Sure, sure, if stedfast meaning,   5
   If single thought could save,
The world might end to-morrow,
   You should not see the grave.

This long and sure-set liking,
   This boundless will to please,   10
– Oh, you should live for ever
   If there were help in these.

But now, since all is idle,
   To this lost heart be kind,
Ere to a town you journey   15
   Where friends are ill to find.

Notes:

"stedfast" – As written. We would write "steadfast."
"single thought" – i.e. a focused, complete thought on a single subject.
"The world might" – i.e., Even if the world should end tomorrow...
"all is idle" – i.e., everything is empty, pointless, worthless.
"a town" – Death is called "a stiller town" in "To an Athlete Dying Young."
"ill to find" – i.e., hard to find.

Guiding Questions:

1. Look at the way in which the lines of stanza one open. What is the significance of the words, "If ... Could ... I think ... Should"?
2. In stanzas two and three what 'forces' does the speaker marshal against the inevitability of the grave?
3. Where does the speaker concede that life is short and death is long? What conclusion about human behavior does he draw from that truth?

Final Thoughts:

   The opposition established in the first stanza, established by alliteration, is between "hearts that **p**erish" and "**p**owers on high" – an obviously unequal match-up. That the speaker knows this is made clear by the qualifications that begin each line, "If ... Could ... I think ... Should." This is all wishful thinking!

In stanza two, we note the contrast between the apparent certainty of, "Sure, sure...," and the hesitation of, "if ... If." Then we realize that, "Sure, sure..." actually means, 'Surely, surely' – it is a plea, not a confident assertion.

Against the inevitability of "the grave" the speaker weighs, "This long and sure-set liking, / This boundless will to please." The words "long" and "boundless" certainly seem as though they might carry some weight, but against the eternity of death they are as nothing – and the speaker knows it, the repetition of "should" and "if" confirm it.

The final stanza begins with a statement of the truth: every hope in the poem has been based upon self-deception. The reality of death makes hopes of immortality "idle," but the speaker urges his companion to understand that in the interim there is a space in which love can be returned. The speaker refers to his "lost heart," suggesting he is in love with his friend. The brevity of life is an argument for returning love for love, because in death "friends are ill to find."

XXXIV   THE NEW MISTRESS

"Oh, sick I am to see you, will you never let me be?
You may be good for something, but you are not good for me.
Oh, go where you are wanted, for you are not wanted here."
And that was all the farewell when I parted from my dear.

"I will go where I am wanted, to a lady born and bred   5
Who will dress me free for nothing in a uniform of red;
She will not be sick to see me if I only keep it clean:
I will go where I am wanted for a soldier of the Queen."

"I will go where I am wanted, for the sergeant does not mind;
He may be sick to see me but he treats me very kind: 10
He gives me beer and breakfast and a ribbon for my cap,
And I never knew a sweetheart spend her money on a chap."

"I will go where I am wanted, where there's room for one or two,
And the men are none too many for the work there is to do;
Where the standing line wears thinner and the dropping dead lie thick; 15
And the enemies of England they shall see me and be sick."

Notes:

"the standing line" – The British Army was famous for its 'thin red line' of troops. The phrase was first used during the Crimean War (October 1853 to February 1856). Standing in line to face the enemy meant that all muskets/rifles could be discharged simultaneously in a volley. This was well attested when, at the climax of the Battle of Waterloo (1815), volley fire from the British lines decimated Napoleon's Old Guard which advanced in columns which meant that only the men in front could return fire.

Guiding Questions:

1. Identify the speaker in the first stanza.
2. Identify the "lady born and bred" mentioned in line 5. What does the protagonist intend to do? How does all this relate to the title of the poem?
3. In what ways does the sergeant treat his men better than any girl ever treated her man?
4. What negative aspects of serving the Queen are acknowledged in stanza four?

Final Thoughts:

The poem begins with the words of a young woman dismissing the speaker at their final meeting. She appears proud and cruel, complaining that he is around her so much that she is "'sick'" of him and telling him bluntly that he is "'not wanted here.'" In her defense, it is clear that the main persona in the poem is head-over-heels in love with a girl who simply does not feel the same way about him. Notice the conscious irony in the phrase "my dear" – it is completely incompatible with the way she ended their relationship. The remaining three stanzas are what the young man said in reply (or perhaps what he wishes he had said) remembered after he "parted from [his] dear."

In stanza two, he gets his revenge by speaking in riddles. He will go, he says, to a "'New Mistress,'" one who is "'a lady born and bred.'" She will clothe him for nothing, and she will not be "'sick to see'" him if only he keeps his clothes clean. The solution to the riddle comes on the final line: his loving mistress is Queen Victoria, and he will become one of her soldiers. Unlike the young woman, who told him, "'you are not wanted here,'" he "'will go where'" he is "'wanted.'" On the surface, this means simply that the Queen is one woman who will always need young men as soldiers, but it also acknowledges that henceforth he will need to go wherever the Empire needs him (Afghanistan, India, South Africa). He will thus lose his freedom.

In stanza three the speaker finds some humor in having substituted the sergeant for a young woman. The sergeant hides his feelings about the recruit. What matters is how the sergeant treats this man: he treats him "'very kind,'" gives him beer and food, "'and a ribbon for my cap.'" The speaker rather enjoys the joke that the Queen's Army will "'spend her money on a chap,'" something he has never known a young woman to do.

In the final stanza, despite his conscious intentions, the speaker acknowledges some problems with the action he proposes. It is true that the Queen wants him, but it is true because she *always* needs men. There is "'room for one or two, / And the men are none too many'" because they keep getting killed. In some part of a foreign field, "'the standing line wears thinner and the dropping dead lie thick.'" Now it is not the girl but "'the enemies of England'" will see him "'and be sick,'" but unlike the girl, they will be firing fatal shots at him.

In sum, this is one of those poems that cleverly qualifies, even undercuts, the words of the speaker/persona. He is blind to the feelings (or lack of feelings) of the young woman and equally blind to the consequences of volunteering for Queen and Country: he has an immature view of love and a naïvely idealistic view of military service. Neither of these views belongs to the poet.

A Shropshire Lad

XXXV

On the idle hill of summer,
  Sleepy with the flow of streams,
Far I hear the steady drummer
  Drumming like a noise in dreams.

Far and near and low and louder   5
  On the roads of earth go by,
Dear to friends and food for powder,
  Soldiers marching, all to die.

East and west on fields forgotten
  Bleach the bones of comrades slain,   10
Lovely lads and dead and rotten;
  None that go return again.

Far the calling bugles hollo,
  High the screaming fife replies,
Gay the files of scarlet follow: 15
  Woman bore me, I will rise.

Notes:

"Drumming ... bugles ... fife": Three musical instruments commonly associated with armies. Remember that it was common until the late nineteenth centuries for troops advancing into battle to be accompanied, even led by, the band.

Guiding Questions:

1. What is it that disturbs the idle tranquility of the rural English summer?
2. In lines 4 to 12, how does the speaker seem to regard the idea of dear friends going for a soldier?
3. What decision does the speaker make in the final stanza?

Final Thoughts:

The most obvious literary technique in stanza one is the use of alliteration. The first two lines combine the long sibilant of the alliterated 's' sound with long, open vowels ("Sleepy ... flow ... streams") while lines three and four combine the urgent, sharp alliterated 'd' sound with short, hard vowels. Thus, the rhythm and sound of the two sets of lines effectively contrasts the description of summer as an "idle" time with the military life which seems to be one of purposive activity. Yet if the word "idle" has negative connotations (and it does), the description of the military drum (perhaps the drum of a squad of recruiters going through the rural villages) is even more so. In a simile, the speaker says it is "like a noise in dreams." Notice the use of the word "noise" rather than, say, 'tune' or 'sound' or 'rhythm.' The fact that it is a "noise" gives the drumming a nightmarish quality

Stanza two qualifies this contrast – to say the least. True, "Soldiers [are] marching," moving purposively along the "roads of earth," while the young man who is not in uniform remains "idle," but the harsh truth is that these men are marching to their deaths. They are, "Dear to friends and food for powder ... all to die." The personification of war as some beast devouring men is hardly original, but remains effective. Suddenly, being "idle" does not seem so bad! Stanza three takes an even more anti-militaristic view. Again, alliteration is used for emphasis. On "fields forgotten / Bleach the bones of ... / Lovely lads." The "rotten" corpses of men strewn, "East and west," are the victims of battles the names of whom no one remembers. Their deaths are thus presented as futile. To ram home the point, line 12 repeats the sentiment of line 8, "None that go return again."

The final stanza marks the triumph of the military spirit – but the speaker's attitude is ambiguous to say the least. The bugles call, but "the screaming fife replies." There is something manic, something irrational, in this reply. The speaker concedes that, "Gay the files of scarlet follow." Note again the use of the hard 'f' alliteration to convey the recruits' determination to do their duty. And see how attractive they look, "Gay ... [in their] scarlet [uniforms]." We note, however, that these dear "friends" and "Lovely lads" have lost their humanity: they have been reduced to "files" (lines of anonymous soldiers). Is the final line optimistic? It seems so. No longer stretched out "idle [on the] hill of summer," the speaker "will rise." The closest thing to a reason is because, "Woman bore me," but that is not a reason. Men go to war, the speaker seems to be saying, because they are born to it, but the speaker has already told us that the men who "rise" to go to war will fall because they "all ... die." The fate of the soldier in Housman's poems is a symbol of the fate of all men: at the height of their youth and vitality, they stoically march toward an inevitably early death.

XXXVI

White in the moon the long road lies,
  The moon stands blank above;
White in the moon the long road lies
  That leads me from my love.

Still hangs the hedge without a gust,   5
  Still, still the shadows stay:
My feet upon the moonlit dust
  Pursue the ceaseless way.

The world is round, so travellers tell,
  And straight though reach the track,   10
Trudge on, trudge on, 'twill all be well,
  The way will guide one back.

But ere the circle homeward hies
  Far, far must it remove:
White in the moon the long road lies   15
  That leads me from my love.

Notes:

Probably the most famous 'road' poem ever is "The Road Not Taken" (1916) by Robert Frost (1874-1963). In that poem, the protagonist has more freedom over the path he chooses and his road certainly does not bring him back home. "hies" – i.e., comes.

Guiding Questions:

1. How does the sound and rhythm of the lines in stanza one compliment their meaning?
2. What do we learn of the speaker's feelings about the path on which he is set?
3. How much consolation do you think he finds in the assurance of travelers that the world is round and will finally bring him back to his beloved?

Final Thoughts:

The speaker describes leaving his beloved. The road lying ahead of him is, "White in the moonlight," and, "The moon stands blank above," suggesting that without the one he loves his landscape is without color and without meaning. The white moon here seems associated with death. Notice the long vowels in the first stanza (particularly the heavy use of the letter 'o') and the alliteration of the long 'l' sound. One senses the speaker's reluctance to set out on the road he knows he must travel in the slow, halting rhythm of the lines.

Stanza two contrasts the stasis of the landscape with the motion (however reluctant and slow) of the speaker's feet. One hears stasis in the long sibilant 's' alliteration of lines 5 and 6. The landscape through which the man tramps is composed of "dust." It is a dead land – dead to him because he must leave the one whom he loves to, "Pursue the ceaseless way." The road, of course, represents his life. He must continue with his life.

The voices of travelers tell him that the "world is round," and therefore that the same road on which he has set out will eventually lead him back to his love, but one senses that the speaker is far from convinced. Even if true, the immediate reality is that he must travel "Far, far" away. The final two lines of the poem repeat the final two lines of stanza one: the speaker's only reality is that now he treads a long road through a white, dusty, dead world.

XXXVII

    As through the wild green hills of Wyre
The train ran, changing sky and shire,
And far behind, a fading crest,
Low in the forsaken west
Sank the high-reared head of Clee,   5
My hand lay empty on my knee.
Aching on my knee it lay:
That morning half a shire away
So many an honest fellow's fist
Had well-nigh wrung it from the wrist.   10
Hand, said I, since now we part
From fields and men we know by heart,
From strangers' faces, strangers' lands,–
Hand, you have held true fellows' hands.
Be clean then; rot before you do   15
A thing they'd not believe of you.
You and I must keep from shame
In London streets the Shropshire name;
On banks of Thames they must not say
Severn breeds worse men than they;   20
And friends abroad must bear in mind
Friends at home they leave behind.
Oh, I shall be stiff and cold
When I forget you, hearts of gold;
The land where I shall mind you not   25
Is the land where all's forgot.
And if my foot returns no more
To Teme nor Corve nor Severn shore,
Luck, my lads, be with you still
By falling stream and standing hill,   30
By chiming tower and whispering tree,
Men that made a man of me.
About your work in town and farm
Still you'll keep my head from harm,
Still you'll help me, hands that gave   35
A grasp to friend me to the grave.

Notes:

"Wyre" – The Wyre Forest straddles the borders of Worcestershire and Shropshire.

Study Guide

"The train ran" – The Tenbury & Bewdley Railway opened in 1864.
"head of Clee" – The Clee Hills are a range in Shropshire that run over 15 miles north-south.
"Teme … Corve … Severn" – The River Corve is a tributary of the River Teme which it joins at Ludlow; the Teme in turn joins the River Severn at Powick near Worcester.

Guiding Questions:

1. The speaker is making a journey. In which direction is he traveling? Where is he going?
2. How does he feel about the journey he is making?
3. What obligation does he feel about the way he will conduct himself in the place to which he is moving?
4. He reflects in the last line that the friends who shook his hand gave him "A grasp to friend me to the grave." Explain what he means by that.

Final Thoughts

This is the first of the exile poems in *A Shropshire Lad* which focus on the differences between the speaker's home shire and London. There is immediately a sense of the speaker leaving a familiar landscape, the features of which he can identify and name. This is "the forsaken west" and his hand, that was that morning shaken vigorously by "many an honest fellow's fist," feels "empty on [his] knee," expressions which suggest his loneliness, loss, sorrow, even guilt, at having deserted his home. Addressing his hand, he urges himself to do nothing with it to bring dishonor on his people. Whether they are friends or strangers, he knows he has "held true fellows' hands" and must do nothing that would "shame" them. He feels it to be his duty to uphold the honor of "the Shropshire name."

Shropshire is presented as an idyllic, rural backwater – a place of "green hills"; of "falling stream and standing hill / … chiming tower and whispering tree"; and of "honest, … true" hardworking fellows with "hearts of gold." He vows to remember it until he dies, "The land where I shall mind you not / Is the land where all's forgot." Moving to London is presented metaphorically, as a kind of dying. The grasp of hands that wished him well become in the last line, "A grasp to friend me to the grave." This sounds negative, but rather it is realistic. Life is a short, one-way journey to the grave, but along the way friendship is a thing of value that makes the experience of existence better.

XXXVIII

The winds out of the west land blow,
  My friends have breathed them there;
Warm with the blood of lads I know
  Comes east the sighing air.

It fanned their temples, filled their lungs,   5
  Scattered their forelocks free;
My friends made words of it with tongues
  That talk no more to me.

Their voices, dying as they fly,
  Thick on the wind are sown;   10
The names of men blow soundless by,
  My fellows' and my own.

Oh lads, at home I heard you plain,
  But here your speech is still,
And down the sighing wind in vain   15
  You hollo from the hill.

The wind and I, we both were there,
  But neither long abode;
Now through the friendless world we fare
  And sigh upon the road.   20

Guiding Questions:

1. What thoughts are generated by the "winds out of the west land"?
2. What is missing from the winds?
3. In what ways does the speaker feel that he and the wind are alike?

Final Thoughts:

The previous poem presented the protagonist's thoughts on the journey to London, but now he is in London (though no town is named). Reminded of his home by a strong west wind which his "friends have breathed" and which is, "Warm with the blood of lads I know," he feels entirely cut off from his roots. The air sighs with regret for the life he has left.

The dense alliteration of the hard 'f' sound in stanza two contributes to a vigorous rhythm that captures the active life of Shropshire lads, but the last line introduces the melancholy tone of stanza three. The voices of these lads "talk no more" to the speaker: the wind simply disperses them. In the wind, he hears only "sighing"; the words of the lads, even their names, are lost.

In the final stanza, the speaker reflects on his short time in Shropshire. Like the wind, he was there, but "neither [he nor the wind] long abode." It is the fate of man and of the wind to move on: nothing is permanent. He now, like the wind, travels "through the friendless world." Shropshire thus resembles the period of childhood, fondly remembered and terribly missed, by the adult who must move on with his life. It is the golden land that exists now only in memory.

XXXIX

'Tis time, I think, by Wenlock town
  The golden broom should blow;
The hawthorn sprinkled up and down
  Should charge the land with snow.

Spring will not wait the loiterer's time   5
  Who keeps so long away;
So others wear the broom and climb
  The hedgerows heaped with may.

Oh tarnish late on Wenlock Edge,
  Gold that I never see;   10
Lie long, high snowdrifts in the hedge
  That will not shower on me.

Notes:

"Wenlock town" – Much Wenlock is a beautiful small town in Shropshire. Its main claim to fame is that The Wenlock Olympian Games, established by Dr William Penny Brookes in 1850, are held in the area. Little Wenlock is a nearby village.
"golden broom" – A kind of shrub or bush.
"hawthorn" – A shrub or small tree with white blossom.

Guiding Questions:

1. What time of year is it?
2. Explain the importance of the repeated word "should" in stanza one.
3. Why will it be "others" who will "wear the broom and climb"?

Final Thoughts:

This is a poem of absent longing. The season is spring and the speaker's thoughts inevitably recreate the scene in Shropshire where the blossoming yellow broom is "golden" and the white hawthorn blossom blown by the wind lies as thick as snow. In stanza two, he laments his continued absence for he knows, "Spring will not wait the loiterer's time." Note the emphasis provided by the alliteration of the strong 'w' sound. He is lamenting a lost opportunity that will neither wait not return. The beauty of the rural scene is captured in the line, "The hedgerows heaped with may." Again, the heavy alliteration suggests the abundance of wildflowers growing in the hedgerows.

He hopes that gold that he will "never see" will "tarnish late" and he hopes that the white hawthorn blossoms will "Lie long" in the hedge bottoms. Yet, he knows that however long they stay they "will not shower on me." This sounds very like a blessing or baptism – one that he will miss. Spring in the countryside is a rebirth, a resurrection, in which he no longer participates for he is in the city.

XL

Into my heart an air that kills
   From yon far country blows:
What are those blue remembered hills,
   What spires, what farms are those?

That is the land of lost content,   5
   I see it shining plain,
The happy highways where I went
   And cannot come again.

Notes:

Read "Nothing Gold Can Stay" (1923) by Robert Frost (1874-1963).
"cannot come again" – Heraclitus, a Greek philosopher born in 544 B.C. explained, "No man ever steps in the same river twice, for it's not the same river and he's not the same man." You will know what he meant if you have ever tried to go back somewhere and recapture a magical moment that you once experienced. It never works! One is always disappointed.

Guiding Questions:

1. What is the "air that kills"?
2. Why do you think that the "remembered hills" are "blue"? Surely hills are green?
3. What is the significance of the question on lines 3 and 4?
4. What new idea about the theme of the poem is introduced in line 5?
5. Why cannot he "come again"?

Final Thoughts:

The speaker feels melancholy nostalgia for a distant land, so distant that he seems to find it hard to remember the names of places he sees in his mind's eye. He identifies it as a place and a time when he was happy, but recognizes sadly that he can never return either to that place or to that innocent state. This is a familiar theme in Housman's poems, but in this poem, it is expressed almost perfectly. The traditional quatrain form, the predominance of monosyllabic words, and the A B A B rhyme scheme are used in many of his poems, but here the simplicity of form, the regularly rhythmic near-perfect quatrains, allow him to deal with a profound theme – the futility of longing for a return to a land and time that is irredeemably past.

There is, however, greater subtlety and depth in the writing than first appears. The opening line, "Into my heart an air that kills," is discordant. The word "air" suggests a very gentle wind, in sharp contrast to the harsh word "kills." Air carries life-giving connotations; it is not associated with killing. There is another level of meaning since the word "air" here is a pun: ostensibly it refers to the wind which is blowing from the lost land, but it also has the meaning of 'a tune or melody.' The point is that the speaker's memory is not merely visual (that is clear enough from stanza one) but also auditory, making it more powerful.

What follows are three visual images: the hills, the spires, and the farms that together encapsulate the idyllic (and quintessentially British) rural nature of the lost land. The memories are, however, not secure. There is something almost desperate in the repletion of the word "what." It is as though the speaker knows that his memories are fading and is trying, rather desperately, to hang on to them. The phrase "blue remembered hills" is quite brilliant, if only because it is so unexpected and original yet so perfectly 'right.' There is no hyphen, so Housman does not intend to imply merely that the speaker is recalling his youth and childhood with a tinge of the blues (i.e., melancholy), although that seems to be a secondary implication. Rather, the hills are blue because they are seen from afar (like the outline of hills on a distant horizon) and because blue is a color strongly associated with tranquility and calm, and we remember that the speaker is 'seeing' these hills not in real time but in his visual memory (i.e., his mind is recreating rather than simply recalling them).

The first line of the second stanza states openly what has only been implied in stanza one: the land about which the speaker feels such a profound sense of loss is not merely a place, it is an earlier period in his life, childhood, when he was "content." Now that he is an adult, life has become more complex. There are inevitably painful memories, missed opportunities, disappointments, bad decisions, etc. In contrast is the perfection of the remembered state, "I see it shining plain." The past shines with purity and simplicity.

Unlike the first stanza, the second makes extensive use of alliteration: "**l**and of **l**ost content," "**h**appy **h**ighways," "**c**annot **c**ome." The sighing 'h' sound of "happy highways" reflects the speaker's futile hope of regaining (or even hanging onto) the past, which the harsher sound of "land of lost content," and "cannot come" convey finality, as does the past tense of "went." The speaker ultimately has to admit that the past is a place to which he "cannot come again"; rather he must go *forward* down life's highway. This was implied when he identified the remembered past in this way, "That is the land of lost content." Had he said 'This' it would have implied that he was back in that land; the word 'that' keeps it at a distance.

Thus, at the start of the poem the speaker cannot quite admit that he is destined always to view his past from an ever-increasing distance. By the last line he has, reluctantly, admitted this truth. The American novelist Thomas Wolfe (1900-1938) wrote a whole novel about it called *You Can't Go Home Again* (1940). The English novelist L. P. Hartley (1895-1972) opens his novel

The Go-Between (1953) with the statement, "The past is a foreign country; they do things differently there."

XLI

        In my own shire, if I was sad
    Homely comforters I had:
    The earth, because my heart was sore,
    Sorrowed for the son she bore;
    And standing hills, long to remain,   5
    Shared their short-lived comrade's pain.
    And bound for the same bourn as I,
    On every road I wandered by,
    Trod beside me, close and dear,
    The beautiful and death-struck year.   10
    Whether in the woodland brown
    I heard the beechnut rustle down,
    And saw the purple crocus pale
    Flower about the autumn dale;
    Or littering far the fields of May   15
    Lady-smocks a-bleaching lay,
    And like a skylit water stood
    The bluebells in the azured wood.

        Yonder, lightening other loads,
    The seasons range the country roads,   20
    But here in London streets I ken
    No such helpmates, only men;
    And these are not in plight to bear,
    If they would, another's care.
    They have enough as 'tis: I see   25
    In many an eye that measures me
    The mortal sickness of a mind
    Too unhappy to be kind.
    Undone with misery, all they can
    Is to hate their fellow man;   30
    And till they drop they needs must still
    Look at you and wish you ill.

Notes:

Although two more different poets are difficult to imagine, read *The Waste Land* (1922) by T. S. Eliot (1888-1965) to find a similar nightmarish vision of London, the quintessential modern city. Granted it is not an easy read, but it is worth it. Here is a brief taster:

        Unreal City,

Under the brown fog of a winter dawn,
A crowd flowed over London Bridge, so many,
I had not thought death had undone so many.
Sighs, short and infrequent, were exhaled,
And each man fixed his eyes before his feet.
Flowed up the hill and down King William Street...

"bourn" – i.e., end, goal, objective.

"Lady-smocks" – *Cardamine pratensis*, colloquially called: cuckooflower, mayflower, and milkmaids, is an attractive wildflower with pale lilac, or occasionally white, petals.

"I ken" – i.e., I know.

"plight" – i.e., condition, circumstances.

Guiding Questions:

1. The speaker gives details of three "homely comforters" in his native shire. What were they? Why and how did they comfort him?
2. What is it that makes the men of the city psychologically incapable of sympathy, empathy and caring for their fellow men?

Final Thoughts:

This poem shows the speaker reflecting on the radical difference he finds between his rural home and the bustling metropolis of London where he is surrounded by a mass of people, none of whom cares for him. Paradoxically, in a city of millions, he has never felt more alone. While other poems concentrate on the different landscapes of Shropshire and London, or on the loss of time past, this poem is a profound comment on the relationship between environment and psychology.

The speaker looks back on his youth with affectionate nostalgia. His life then was not innocent: he suffered "pain" and was "sad." However, Shropshire is presented as having been nurturing. The "homely comforters" are: mother earth, because she "bore" him; the hills, because in him they saw a "short-lived comrade"; the cycle of the year, because it knew itself to be, like him, moving to an end, which was expressed in the beautiful flora. The earth is personified as the immortal Earth Mother; the hills are personified as "comrades," soldiers who care for a fellow soldier whom they sense has not long to live; the year is personified as a fellow-traveler, "close and dear," whose seasons are like the stages of human life, and equally finite. Thus, the first stanza depends upon the pathetic fallacy, the attribution of human feelings and responses to inanimate things or animals.

In the second stanza, the speaker makes the contrast between, "Yonder" and "here in London." Here there are not "country roads" but only "streets"; here

Nature's "helpmates" are absent and there are only "men," men whose lives make them incapable of sharing "another's care." These men suffer, "The mortal sickness of a mind / Too unhappy to be kind." Overwhelmed by their own misery, they can only warily assess ("measure") their fellow men, "hate" them and will them "ill."

The anthropomorphism (i.e., the attribution of human traits, emotions, or intentions to non-human entities) of stanza one is uncharacteristic of Housman alerting readers to the element of unrealistic nostalgia in the recollections of the exiled speaker. He looks back on his youth in Shropshire through rose-tinted spectacles and sees it as the idyll it never was. The poems I-XXXVI describe Shropshire (the land of lost content) very differently from the poems of exile which begin with XXXVII.

XLII   THE MERRY GUIDE

Once in the wind of morning
  I ranged the thymy wold;
The world-wide air was azure
  And all the brooks ran gold.

There through the dews beside me   5
  Behold a youth that trod,
With feathered cap on forehead,
  And poised a golden rod.

With mien to match the morning
  And gay delightful guise   10
And friendly brows and laughter
  He looked me in the eyes.

Oh whence, I asked, and whither?
  He smiled and would not say,
And looked at me and beckoned   15
  And laughed and led the way.

And with kind looks and laughter
  And nought to say beside
We two went on together,
  I and my happy guide.   20

Across the glittering pastures
  And empty upland still
And solitude of shepherds
  High in the folded hill,

By hanging woods and hamlets   25
  That gaze through orchards down
On many a windmill turning
  And far-discovered town,

With gay regards of promise
  And sure unslackened stride   30
And smiles and nothing spoken
  Led on my merry guide.

By blowing realms of woodland
    With sunstruck vanes afield
And cloud-led shadows sailing   35
    About the windy weald,

By valley-guarded granges
    And silver waters wide,
Content at heart I followed
    With my delightful guide.   40

And like the cloudy shadows
    Across the country blown
We two face on for ever,
    But not we two alone.

With the great gale we journey   45
    That breathes from gardens thinned,
Borne in the drift of blossoms
    Whose petals throng the wind;

Buoyed on the heaven-heard whisper
    Of dancing leaflets whirled   50
From all the woods that autumn
    Bereaves in all the world.

And midst the fluttering legion
    Of all that ever died
I follow, and before us   55
    Goes the delightful guide,

With lips that brim with laughter
    But never once respond,
And feet that fly on feathers,
    And serpent-circled wand.   60

Notes:

"thymy wold" – Thyme is a flowering herb. Wolds are high, open, uncultivated moorland where thyme grows wild.

"a golden rod." – Goldenrod is a yellow flowering perennial plant with healing properties.

"mien" – i.e., way of behaving, air, bearing, demeanor.

"leaflets" – i.e., small leaves.

"Bereaves" – i.e., separates through their death.

Guiding Questions:

1. Comment on the setting described in the first stanza.
2. What do we learn in stanzas two to five about the person who is leading the speaker?
3. What features of the landscape are emphasized in stanzas six to ten?
4. In what ways does the description of the two people walking change radically from stanza eleven on?
5. Who is the silent guide? Support your answer by reference to the text.

Final Thoughts:

The speaker remembers one particular morning when he walked over the moors. He describes a perfect day that delighted the senses: the wind on his skin, the color and smell of the thyme, the blue of the sky, and the gold of the brooks.

In stanza two we learn that the speaker was accompanied by another person whom he calls "my happy guide." We know that this was a mysterious figure, even to the speaker at the time, because he asks this companion, "Oh whence ... and whither?" but to this question he gets no answer. There is nothing threatening about this stranger: he smiles, laughs, beckons and looks on the speaker kindly, thereby winning his confidence. Though it is not said, the reader realizes the guide is a nature spirit. The speaker is remembering another day that seemed perfect for a hike back when he was a youth, and this is what leads him on to ramble now.

Stanzas six to ten give a detailed account of the landscape through which the two walk that morning. Everything seems perfect and the speaker projects his happiness onto his still-silent companion calling him "my delightful guide."

Stanzas eleven to fifteen continue the description of the walk, but there is a change. Somehow this is no longer a description of a single walk on a particular day but of a life-experience, "We two fare on for ever." And the two no longer seem to be walking but drifting "like the cloudy shadows / Across the country blown." They are suddenly part of the natural world through which they journey, carried like "the drift of blossoms" by the wind. Thus, the speaker dramatically asserts, "like the cloudy shadows / Across the country blown / We two fare on for ever." They have become a part of everything that ever lived and therefore of "all that ever died" – a mystical belief in the oneness of things.

It becomes clear that the speaker is not merely talking about a walk in a particular place on a particular day; he is describing the journey of his life in which he is led by the incarnate spirit of the Shropshire landscape.

XLIII THE IMMORTAL PART

When I meet the morning beam,
Or lay me down at night to dream,
I hear my bones within me say,
"Another night, another day."

"When shall this slough of sense be cast,   5
This dust of thoughts be laid at last,
The man of flesh and soul be slain
And the man of bone remain?"

"This tongue that talks, these lungs that shout,
These thews that hustle us about,   10
This brain that fills the skull with schemes,
And its humming hive of dreams,–"

"These to-day are proud in power
And lord it in their little hour:
The immortal bones obey control   15
Of dying flesh and dying soul."

"'Tis long till eve and morn are gone:
Slow the endless night comes on,
And late to fulness grows the birth
That shall last as long as earth."   20

"Wanderers eastward, wanderers west,
Know you why you cannot rest?
'Tis that every mother's son
Travails with a skeleton."

"Lie down in the bed of dust;   25
Bear the fruit that bear you must;
Bring the eternal seed to light,
And morn is all the same as night."

"Rest you so from trouble sore,
Fear the heat o' the sun no more,   30
Nor the snowing winter wild,
Now you labour not with child."
"Empty vessel, garment cast,
We that wore you long shall last.

– Another night, another day."   35
So my bones within me say.

Therefore they shall do my will
To-day while I am master still,
And flesh and soul, now both are strong,
Shall hale the sullen slaves along,   40

Before this fire of sense decay,
This smoke of thought blow clean away,
And leave with ancient night alone
The stedfast and enduring bone.

Notes:

"slough of sense" – To 'slough off' means to get rid of something, as a snake sloughs off (discards) its dead skin. If you slough something off, you treat it as unimportant. In this case, the bones look forward to the time they will discard the flesh and the consciousness that it enables.

"thews" – i.e. the muscles and tendons giving strength to the body.

"travails" – i.e., labors painfully.

"hale" – i.e., drag or pull.

Guiding Questions:

1. What is the attitude of the bones to the "flesh and soul" that they support?

2. Analyze the metaphor of the "'humming hive of dreams.'" (What is being compared to what? Comment on the points of similarity. How effective is the comparison?)

3. Analyze the metaphor, "'late to fulness grows the birth / That shall last as long as earth.'"

4. Analyze the metaphor, "'Empty vessel, garment cast.'"

5. Analyze the metaphor of "'the eternal seed.'"

6. Describe the tone of the last two stanzas. How does the speaker respond to what his bones have said?

Final Thoughts:

The highly original conceit upon which this poem is built is clearly explained by Cleanth Brooks:

> [T]he speaker perversely insists that the immortal part of man is
> his skeleton – not the spirit, not the soul – but the most earthly,
> the most mineral part of his body. The bones will endure long
> after the "dust of thoughts" has at last been laid and the flesh

itself has become dust. The device on which the poem is built is the grumbling complaint of the bones ... counting the days of their servitude and predicting the day of their deliverance in which the flesh will fall away from them and leave them free and unfettered. ("Alfred Edward Housman," in Ricks Ed. 70).

The poem is a dialogue. The first voice we hear is that of the man who reports that he hears the second voice morning and evening. The evocation of morning is given vitality by the 'm' alliteration ("When I **meet** the **morning** bea**m**") and by the irregular rhythm (the iambic is disrupted by the absence of the third unstressed syllable, giving a seven-syllable line: "When **I meet** the **morn**ing beam"). In contrast, the calm of evening is conveyed by the dull 'd' alliteration, ("Or lay me **d**own at night to **d**ream"), the conventional phrase "lay me down," and the completely regular iambic line ("Or **lay** me **down** at **night** to **dream**").

The first words of the bones, "'Another night, another day'" suggest a cyclical, essentially static view of life (something like the movie "Groundhog Day") in which nothing changes and nothing is achieved. In another poem Housman will use the image of life as a treadmill, and that same depressing idea is captured here. The bones know that they will outlast consciousness (which will disappear at the moment of death) and the flesh (which will decompose more gradually), but at present they feel constrained and limited by their attachment to these things. The bones imagine casting them off and thereby being liberated. You can hear the sneering contempt in the spitting 's' alliteration of the phrase, "'slough of sense.'"

The third stanza stresses the agency of the mind and the flesh through the use of active verbs, "'talks ... hustle ... fills,'" presenting the bones as helpless. Notice the force of the strong 't' alliteration in "'tongue that talks.'" This idea is captured in a brilliant metaphor of the skull as an empty bee hive that the brain sets "humming" with its dreams, just as a beekeeper might place a swarm of bees in a hive. The next stanza qualifies the agency of the mind and the flesh. They are "'proud in power,'" the stress falling on the two monosyllables and augmented by the strong 'p' alliteration. However, the word "to-day" implies that their power is time-limited. This leads to the mocking assertion that they "'lord it in their little hour.'" Now the alliteration works to support the message of the bones. There is a comic disparity between the arrogance of the mind and flesh and the shortness of their period of agency. This leads naturally to the clear statement of the paradox that the bones see, "'The immortal bones obey control / Of dying flesh and dying soul.'" The contrast between immortal and dying brings home what the bones see as the true relationship between the two.

Stanza four leads to an even more audacious metaphor: for the bones, death will be a "'birth.'" The bones lament the frustrating slowness of time in passing before this birth to freedom, "''Tis long till ... Slow the endless night ...late to fullness...,'" but they know that the birth that will eventually come "'shall last as long as earth.'" In the battle between mortal time and eternity there can be only one winner. It is the essence of the human condition, the bones say, that "every mother's son / Travails with a skeleton." Housman here uses a pun on travels/travails: the human journey is a battle in which the mind and flesh are opposed by the one thing that will outlive them.

Stanza six includes another audacious metaphor: when the dead body is planted in the ground, it will, "'Bear the fruit that bear [it] must.'" Dying will put an end to the mortal flesh and consciousness and bring to light the "'eternal seed.'" This is not, as we might conventionally expect, the immortal soul of Christian faith but the structure of bones that "wore" those things that have now been cast aside like an, "'Empty vessel, [or a] garment.'" In the grave, the bones, "'Rest ... from trouble sore'"; suffering neither from summer heat nor winter cold. They "'labour not with child'" – another startlingly original metaphor. The bones compare themselves in life to a woman in constant labor (a very painful process), always struggling to 'give birth' to the desires of the mind and the flesh. Now, in death, the skeleton is freed from this painful conflict.

In the last two stanzas, Cleanth Brooks points out, Housman introduces "a brilliant shift in tone ... The man answers back ... The human spirit is given its due. The worst has been faced down, though not denied" (*Ibid.* 71). The tone of these two stanzas is defiant: "flesh and soul" are, for the moment "strong"; they are the "master" and the bones "the sullen slaves." The speaker vows to make the bones bend to his "will" before the inevitable end. Nor does he see the moment of death as the liberation that the bones anticipate. True they are steadfast and will endure longer than the mind and flesh, but their fate is to be left "with ancient night alone" – an eternity of darkness.

The attraction of this poem lies in its sheer audacity and (something that can seldom be said of Housman) in the wit of his imagery. There is a good case for calling this comic verse, but the comedy exists to provoke the reader to rethink conventional ideas.

XLIV

Shot? so quick, so clean an ending?
   Oh that was right, lad, that was brave:
Yours was not an ill for mending,
   'Twas best to take it to the grave.

Oh you had forethought, you could reason,   5
   And saw your road and where it led,
And early wise and brave in season
   Put the pistol to your head.

Oh soon, and better so than later
   After long disgrace and scorn,   10
You shot dead the household traitor,
   The soul that should not have been born.

Right you guessed the rising morrow
   And scorned to tread the mire you must:
Dust's your wages, son of sorrow,   15
   But men may come to worse than dust.

Souls undone, undoing others,–
   Long time since the tale began.
You would not live to wrong your brothers:
   Oh lad, you died as fits a man.   20

Now to your grave shall friend and stranger
   With ruth and some with envy come:
Undishonoured, clear of danger,
   Clean of guilt, pass hence and home.

Turn safe to rest, no dreams, no waking;   25
   And here, man, here's the wreath I've made:
'Tis not a gift that's worth the taking,
   But wear it and it will not fade.

Notes:

This poem and the next were inspired by the suicide of a nineteen-year-old naval cadet at Woolwich on August 6th, 1895. We know this because Housman clipped a newspaper article on the suicide and left it in his copy of *A Shropshire Lad* at precisely this point. In the article, the young man's suicide note (actually a long letter to the Coroner explaining his action) was quoted. Laurence Housman wrote, "It is quite evident that certain passages in that letter prompted the writing of the poem; one sentence indeed is almost quoted" (quoted in Leggett *Theme and Structure* 92). The cadet began by saying, "I wish it to be clearly understood that I am not what is commonly called 'temporarily insane' and that I am putting an end to my life after several weeks of careful deliberation." He then gave two reasons for his determination to end his life. The first was that, "there is only one thing in this world that would make me thoroughly happy; that one thing I have no earthly hope of attaining," and the second that "I have absolutely ruined my own life; but I thank God that as yet ... I have not morally injured ... anyone else." The cadet concluded that he has decided to take his own life rather than live "a long series of ... disgraces" (*Ibid.*). Though sexuality is never mentioned, the implications of the cadet's words are clear.

"ruth" – i.e., a feeling of pity, distress, or grief.

Guiding Questions:

1. Why, in the first paragraph, does the speaker approve of the man having shot himself?
2. What additional reason for approval is given in stanza two?
3. What do you understand the speaker to mean by the phrase "the household traitor"?
4. In stanzas three and four, what is suggested to be "worse than [coming to] dust"?
5. What noble motive is attributed to the man who committed suicide in stanza five?
6. Why, according to the speaker in stanza six, will some who visit the man's grave envy him?
7. What is the "wreath" that the speaker offers?
8. So this is a poem expressing approval for a young man who shot himself because he feared that he was gay. Right?

Final Thoughts:

In his essay "The Land of Lost Content: Housman's Shropshire," Peter Firchow has this comment on the poem:

> Astonishing advice! Homosexuals of the world, Housman seems to be saying, dispatch yourself ... What this enthusiastic endorsement of this youth's suicide seems to suggest is that Housman never really grew up ... Housman may not have killed himself when he perceived the growth of a 'disease' in his own soul, but he did undertake radical emotional surgery which left him maimed for the remainder of his life. (Firchow *et al.* 22)

How accurate Firchow might be in his comments of Housman's own life is outside my scope and expertise. However, such an interpretation of this poem depends upon taking the words of the speaker literally and assuming that the voice we hear is that of the author (always a problematic assumption). I am not able to do that because I find Housman's poem to be heavily ironic. As a gay man, Housman's reaction to the cadet's suicide was complex, but the ostensible reaction of this poem is simple – not to say simplistic. The voice we here is that of 'the (heterosexual) establishment' undercut at every turn by the author's irony.

In the first two lines, death by shooting is described as "quick ... clean ... right ... brave." These epithets are questionable at best; at worst they are the sort of nonsense spouted by the same sort of people whom Wilfred Owen was attacking when he mocked, "The old Lie: *Dulce et decorum est / Pro patria mori.*" The voice in the poem is neither that of Housman nor Terence, but of someone incapable of either sympathy or empathy, or even of feeling pity for a young man who finds himself attracted to other young men in a world that insists that he must be attracted to young women and condemns his urges as unnatural, sinful and criminal.

The mock approval in the next two lines satirizes the British concept of a gentleman's honor, of 'doing the right thing.' The reader knows this because the whole expression is too glib ever to be taken at face value: it is parody. Look at the facile rhymes of stanza two (particularly "led ... head"). It is true that Housman almost always uses full rhymes and favors monosyllables, leading to a fair number of jangling rhymes, but anyone unconvinced by this reading should consider the statement, "men may come to worse than dust." A reader of *A Shropshire Lad* must immediately want to cry out, "There is nothing worse than dust! No there isn't!" for the entire thrust of the poem cycle is that life is immensely valuable *because* it is short and full of sorrow, and *because* our hold on it is so fragile, and *because* eternity is so long. To take another example, the line, "Turn safe to rest, no dreams, no waking," is self-contradictory, for waking and dreaming are positive aspects of life, not things that prevent us from resting (that would be labor or suffering or heart ache or nightmares). In killing himself this young man has killed his dreams and wakings.

In the final stanza, Housman almost comes clean about his intention, labelling his own poem a "wreath I've made: / [That] is not a gift that's worth the taking." He is referencing the wreath's used at official memorials to the dead by which the great and the good recognize the sacrifices of those who have given their lives for their country. Such gestures are for show; they lack real knowledge of those they commemorate. These lines are a blast against people who cannot simply look the other way but feel they must condemn a young man whose only sin is to love; people who believe that such a man has a "soul that should not have been born." That statement is patently absurd. For one thing, his soul obviously *was* born. For another, it must have been born as it was by God's will, otherwise God cannot be omnipotent.

On my reading, then, this poem is a satire – not, to be sure, of the tragic young man, but of the society that indoctrinated him into believing that being a gay man he had no right to live and owed it to the rest of society to 'do the honorable thing.' Housman excelled at this kind of satire his whole life both in his writing, his teaching and his interactions with friends: his readers, students, acquaintances and friends were frequently so much in awe of his reserved and serious reputation that they did not get the joke. We ought not to make the same mistake with this poem.

XLV

> If it chance your eye offend you,
>> Pluck it out, lad, and be sound:
> 'Twill hurt, but here are salves to friend you,
>> And many a balsam grows on ground.
>
> And if your hand or foot offend you,   5
>> Cut it off, lad, and be whole;
> But play the man, stand up and end you,
>> When your sickness is your soul.

Notes:

Take a break! Got to YouTube and search, "The Black Knight *Monty Python and the Holy Grail.*" When you have read the poem, you will see the significance. The poem references the following statements from Jesus's Sermon on the Mount:

> And if thy right eye offend thee, pluck it out, and cast it from thee: for it is profitable for thee that one of thy members should perish, and not that thy whole body should be cast into hell. And if thy right hand offend thee, cut it off, and cast it from thee: for it is profitable for thee that one of thy members should perish, and not that thy whole body should be cast into hell. (*Matthew* 5.29-30 King James Version)

"salves" – i.e., a soothing ointment or balm.
"balsam" – i.e., a resin substance exuded by certain trees and shrubs used as a base for medical balms.

Guiding Questions:

1. What consolations are offered in stanza one to a lad who will (metaphorically speaking) pluck out his eye?
2. What consolations are offered in stanza two to a lad who will (metaphorically speaking) cut off his hand or foot?
3. How consoling do *you* find these consolations?

Final Thoughts:

How does satire work? Let us briefly take the example of *A Modest Proposal For preventing the Children of Poor People From being a Burthen to Their Parents or Country, and For making them Beneficial to the Publick* (1729) by Jonathan Swift (1667-1745). The modest proposal is, of course, that the poor should eat their children because, "A young healthy child well nursed, is, at a year old, a most delicious nourishing and wholesome food, whether stewed, roasted, baked, or boiled; and I make no doubt that it will equally serve in a fricassee, or a ragout." The entire point of Swift's satire is in the serious tone with which absurdity is spoken, so how do we know that, as readers, we are to understand that the author is satirizing not only the ideas in the proposal but more widely the attitude of the conservative establishment to the condition of the poor? In a word, we know because what is proposed is self-evidently *absurd*.

It is the same with this poem. Plucking out your eye will, we are told in all seriousness, "hurt" – which strikes the reader as something of an understatement. Plucking out your eye will, we are told in all seriousness, make you "sound" – which strikes the reader as oxymoronic since plucking out your eye tends to make you blind (at least in that eye). Similarly, cutting your hand or foot off, we are told, will make you "whole" – which it self-evidently will not since you will be minus a hand or foot. Actually, if you keep going, there will be nothing left of you!

Housman follows these absurdities with the cliché, "play the man." This is the sort of thing characters say in very old British movies about war when a man shows what is perceived to be weakness (generally by evincing a desire to keep on living instead of going down fighting in a hopeless cause). Here the emphasis of the speaker is on moral weakness because the phrase means 'play the man God created you to be.' It also echoes these lines from "Vitae Lampada" (1892) by Sir Henry John Newbolt (1862-1938)"

The river of death has brimmed his banks,
And England's far, and Honour a name,
But the voice of a schoolboy rallies the ranks:
"Play up! play up! and play the game!"

The key word in Housman's line is "play" because it is so evidently the wrong word – life and death, particularly by suicide, are not a game to be played. This is followed by the oxymoronic, "stand up and end you," which is, of course, a contradiction in terms since in shooting yourself you are standing up so that you will fall down. In the last two lines, the speaker follows the logic of the argument to its conclusion: if God wants us to pluck out a defective eye or chop off an offensive hand or foot, then if the soul is the thing that is sick, He obviously wants you to kill yourself. This is as patently absurd a remedy as is the poor eating their children. Not only does it violate the Commandment, "Thou shalt not kill" (*Exodus* 20.13 King James Version), but the Church has for centuries denied Christian burial for suicides.

If the reader remains in any doubt as to how this poem should be understood, recall that Housman was a self-avowed atheist (albeit one brought up in High Church Anglicanism and immensely well read in Christian texts). In this poem, which ostensibly recommends suicide for any man who feels shameful gay impulses, he uses a text which, in context, refers to men who feel shameful heterosexual impulses. These are the two verses that precede those quoted in the Notes above:

> Ye have heard that it was said by them of old time, Thou shalt not commit adultery: But I say unto you, That whosoever looketh on a woman to lust after her hath committed adultery with her already in his heart. (*Matthew* 5.27-28 King James Version)

In conclusion, I cannot resist answering Peter Firchow (see above). No doubt A. E. Housman was in many ways a strange chap who kept his emotions firmly in check. I can find not the slightest evidence, however, that he was ever conflicted about his own sexuality. Housman seems to have been, in himself, quite happily gay; we must look elsewhere for the origin of the "radical emotional surgery" which Firchow identifies. [I would suggest in the early death of his mother, his academic failure and the inability of the one person he ever loved to return his feelings.]

XLVI

Bring, in this timeless grave to throw,
No cypress, sombre on the snow;
Snap not from the bitter yew
His leaves that live December through;
Break no rosemary, bright with rime   5
And sparkling to the cruel clime;
Nor plod the winter land to look
For willows in the icy brook
To cast them leafless round him: bring
No spray that ever buds in spring.   10

But if the Christmas field has kept
Awns the last gleaner overstept,
Or shrivelled flax, whose flower is blue
A single season, never two;
Or if one haulm whose year is o'er   15
Shivers on the upland frore,
– Oh, bring from hill and stream and plain
Whatever will not flower again,
To give him comfort: he and those
Shall bide eternal bedfellows   20
Where low upon the couch he lies
Whence he never shall arise.

Notes:

"cypress" – An evergreen coniferous tree which is a symbol of mourning, immortality, elevation and hope.

"somber" – i.e., dark, gloomy, solemn.

"yew" – An evergreen tree or shrub with red berries. It is symbolic of immortality and everlasting life, rebirth, changes and regeneration after difficult times, and protection.

"rosemary" – An aromatic evergreen shrub with blue flowers. It is a symbol of friendship, loyalty, and remembrance. Rosemary is traditionally carried by mourners at funerals. The mad Ophelia lamenting the death of Polonius her father says, "There's rosemary, that's for remembrance. Pray you, love, remember" (*Hamlet* Act 4 Scene 5).

"rime" – i.e., accumulated crystals of frost.

"willows" – The willow is a deciduous tree or shrub, scattering long, thin leaves each fall. "Green, like the leaves on the branches, symbolizes nature, fertility, and life. It also represents balance, learning, growth, and harmony. Our image of the willow tree represents the strength, stability, and structure of the trunk, standing firm and withstanding the greatest of challenges" ("The Symbolism of the Willow Tree," willowplaceforwomen.com).

"spray" – i.e., a flowering branch or shoot.

"ever" – i.e., always.

"Awns" – i.e., stiff bristles growing from the ear or flower of barley, rye, and many grasses.

"gleaner" – i.e., someone who picks up strands of grain left in the field by the harvesters (who would have been using scythes not more efficient harvesting machinery).

"flax" – A blue flowered herbaceous plant cultivated for its edible seed and for textile fiber made from its stalks.

"haulm" – i.e., a stalk or stem.

"frore" – i.e., frozen or frosty.

Guiding Questions:

1. What do you understand by the phrase, "timeless grave"?
2. Why does the speaker want none of the plants mentioned to be thrown into the grave? What do they have in common?
3. What kind of plants does the speaker want to go into the grave? What do they have in common?

Final Thoughts:

The syntax of the opening instructions is unusual and at first difficult to understand. The poem begins with an imperative, "Bring" but only on the second line is this countermanded by the negative, "No." This single negative is followed by a whole string of negatives: "Snap not … no … Nor plod … No…" The reader soon understands that the plants mentioned are those that people might be expected to bring to a funeral. With the exception of the willow, all of the named plants are evergreens that do not die back in winter. Even more importantly, these are plants that have (across many cultures) connotations of immortality, remembrance and/or strength. The speaker wants his friend to lie in his grave with plants other than these because he has no faith in life after death.

Stanza two begins with a list of three plants that he thinks would be appropriate. Each one "will not flower again," just as the speaker's friend will not live again, either in this world or the next. Even mentioning it, the Christian idea of resurrection to the life to come has been discounted. Now the imperative is much stronger, "– Oh, bring." It is an exhortation. Only then does the reader learn that this speaker is reacting to a death that has happened very recently – the body of the friend is still lying on the couch where (presumably) he had gone to lie because he was feeling unwell.

XLVII   THE CARPENTER'S SON

"Here the hangman stops his cart:
Now the best of friends must part.
Fare you well, for ill fare I:
Live, lads, and I will die."

"Oh, at home had I but stayed   5
'Prenticed to my father's trade,
Had I stuck to plane and adze,
I had not been lost, my lads."

"Then I might have built perhaps
Gallows-trees for other chaps,   10
Never dangled on my own,
Had I but left ill alone."

"Now, you see, they hang me high,
And the people passing by
Stop to shake their fists and curse;   15
So 'tis come from ill to worse."

"Here hang I, and right and left
Two poor fellows hang for theft:
All the same's the luck we prove,
Though the midmost hangs for love."   20

"Comrades all, that stand and gaze,
Walk henceforth in other ways;
See my neck and save your own:
Comrades all, leave ill alone."

"Make some day a decent end,   25
Shrewder fellows than your friend.
Fare you well, for ill fare I:
Live, lads, and I will die."

Notes:

Since this poem describes a public hanging, it is important to know that public executions for murder in the United Kingdom were ended in 1868 by Act of Parliament. Henceforth, all executions occurred, and the bodies were buried, within the prison grounds. Charles Dickens (1812-1870) witnessed a public hanging and wrote about it.

"at home had I but stayed / 'Prenticed to my father's trade" – The earthly father of Jesus was Joseph who is called in the Gospels a carpenter by profession. The story is told that when he was twelve Jesus visited Jerusalem with Joseph and Mary. Actually, they left to return home to Nazareth thinking he was with someone else in their group, but when they discovered he was not they returned and found him in the Temple debating with the learned men. They were both amazed and a bit angry, but he turned to them and said:

> How is it that ye sought me? wist ye not that I must be about my
> Father's business? And they understood not the saying which he
> spake unto them. (*Luke* 2. 49-50 King James Version)

"adze" – An axe-like tool with an arched blade at right angles to the handle, used for shaping wood.

"the people passing by / Stop to shake their fists and curse" – Compare:

> Pilate saith unto them, "What shall I do then with Jesus which is
> called Christ?" They all say unto him, "Let him be crucified."
> And the governor said, "Why, what evil hath he done?" But they
> cried out the more, saying, "Let him be crucified." ... And they
> spit upon him, and took the reed, and smote him on the head.
> And after that they had mocked him, they took the robe off from
> him, and put his own raiment on him, and led him away to
> crucify him. (*Matthew* 27. 22-32 King James Version)

"Two poor fellows hang for theft" – Compare:

> Then were there two thieves crucified with him, one on the right
> hand, and another on the left. And they that passed by reviled
> him, wagging their heads ... (*Matthew* 27. 38-39 King James
> Version)

Guiding Questions:

1. There is plenty of detail in the poem that associates the speaker with Jesus Christ. Is there anything that suggests he is *not* Jesus?

2. Suggest at least two interpretations of the line, "Had I but left ill alone."

3. Suggest at least two interpretations of the phrase, "the midmost hangs for love."

4. What is the speaker's final advice to the friends whom he leaves behind?

Final Thoughts:

It is a central tenant of the Christian faith that by dying on the cross Jesus the Christ took upon himself the sins of men (which had their origin in Adam and Eve defying God by eating the fruit of the Tree of Knowledge) so that all who believed in him would receive mercy and salvation. Christ died that we might have eternal life by our faith in Him and his Resurrection. In the first stanza, Housman alludes this belief when his speaker says, "'Fare you well, for ill fare I: / Live lads, and I will die'" – lines repeated at the end of the poem.

However, the voice in Housman's poem is *not* that of the Christ – or at least it is not that of the divine Christ described in the *New Testament*. To state the obvious, the persona in the poem is being hung in England and in public, presumably at a crossroads ("Here the hangman stops his cart"). Also, the poem describes the persona only as a carpenter's son, a mortal being. There is no suggestion that he is the Son of God. That said, the parallels with Jesus are exact and deliberate (as the Notes above make clear). The speaker laments his misfortune wishing that he had lived his life differently. Superficially, this is rather like Jesus's call to God in the Garden of Gethsemane, "O my Father, if it be possible, let this cup pass from me" (*Matthew* 26. 39 King James Version). However, his thought that had he "stuck to plane and adze" then he "might have built perhaps / Gallows-trees for other chaps" is definitely un-Christ-like.

The crux of the poem lies in the ambiguity of the speaker's conviction that he would have, "Never dangled on my own, / Had I but left ill alone." Does "left ill alone" mean that he should have avoided breaking the law or that he should have ignored the many evils of society? The violent reactions of the people who have come to see him executed described in stanza four, would fit with either interpretation. Housman was well aware that social reformers such as the suffragettes clamoring for the vote or pacifists who opposed wars in his own day generated passionate opposition among social conservatives (and he was honest enough to have known this even although he would have called himself a social conservative who opposed votes for women and supported British wars). The ambiguity is resolved somewhat, when the speaker announces that, unlike the thieves hanging on either side of him, "the midmost hangs for love." This rules out the idea that the man is being punished for a life of crime (at least in the conventional sense). He is either being hung because his altruistic sense led him into conflict with the establishment or (and this is a new idea in the poem) because he was gay and society criminalized him. Remember that, in England and Wales, it was not until 1967 that the Sexual Offences Bill decriminalized homosexual acts between two men over twenty-one years of age in private.

Stanza six makes it clear that Housman's persona can, like Christ, die that others might live, but not in any miraculous sense. Instead, the speaker tells others to learn from his example, "See my neck and save your own." Saving one's neck is somewhat more down to earth than the concept of eternal salvation! Leggett comments on the significance of the speaker:

> Housman's Christ is a disillusioned man who is faced with the vanity of his efforts in the light of his knowledge of the true nature of man. As Andrews notes, the lesson Housman draws from the life of Christ is that it is futile to attempt to change

man's nature, to war with evil; the mature man has learned to accept it as an inevitable condition in a transitory and imperfect world. Housman's Christ has accepted at his death the essential mortality of man, and the only promise he is able to leave to his comrades is that they will face a better death than he now faces. (*Theme and Structure* 42)

No brave martyr to the gay cause, the speaker counsels his friends to live an ostensibly 'normal' (i.e., straight) life that does not challenge the norms of society. He urges them to, "Walk henceforth in other ways." This advice is pragmatic: be "Shrewder fellows than your friend," he urges and "leave ill alone," and, "Make some day a decent end."

Many critics interpret this poem as a satire against Jesus, but I can find nothing in Housman's life or thought that would make him want to satirize Jesus and certainly nothing in the poem to suggest that is his intention. I am normally skeptical of interpreting texts on the basis of the author's biography, but in this case I will make an exception. Housman's mother and his step-mother, both of whom he loved and respected, were women of faith. Housman once referred to himself as a "High Church atheist" explaining that he had been brought up in that Christian tradition despite his personal loss of faith. It is frankly inconceivable that Housman would have satirized the central tenant of his mothers' faith, even if it was one in which he could not himself believe. The speaker is neither Jesus nor Housman. The speaker is a modern-day, secular Christ-figure who dies because he loves his fellow man rather than his fellow woman. As a gay man, Housman knew that in England he had to suppress his sexual impulses. (On the Continent, he was able to follow his sexual preferences more openly and with less fear of prosecution – and did so.) The man who had lived through the shaming and destruction of Oscar Wilde (to whom he sent a copy of *A Shropshire Lad* when Wilde was in prison), knew that he had to adopt the public persona of the irreproachable Professor of Latin. From the writing in the poem, he had a great deal of sympathy with his weak and repentant persona, but that does not mean that he himself was either weak or repentant about his sexual orientation.

XLVIII

Be still, my soul, be still; the arms you bear are brittle,
　Earth and high heaven are fixt of old and founded strong.
Think rather,– call to thought, if now you grieve a little,
　The days when we had rest, O soul, for they were long.

Men loved unkindness then, but lightless in the quarry　　　5
　I slept and saw not; tears fell down, I did not mourn;
Sweat ran and blood sprang out and I was never sorry:
　Then it was well with me, in days ere I was born.

Now, and I muse for why and never find the reason,
　I pace the earth, and drink the air, and feel the sun.　　　10
Be still, be still, my soul; it is but for a season:
　Let us endure an hour and see injustice done.

Ay, look: high heaven and earth ail from the prime foundation;
　All thoughts to rive the heart are here, and all are vain:
Horror and scorn and hate and fear and indignation –　　　15
　Oh why did I awake? when shall I sleep again?

Notes:

Read the poem "They Are Not Long" (1896) by Ernest Dowson (1867-1900) which has a similar theme. It begins with a Latin quotation which means, "The shortness of life prevents us from entertaining far-off hopes." Dowson's own life was tragically short.
"arms" – i.e., weapons.
"fixt" – i.e., fixed, firm.
"in the quarry" – i.e., he was then earth, before he was formed into a man at birth.
"ere" – i.e., before.
"muse" – i.e., think, reflect.
"rive" – i.e., split, crack or tear apart violently. Apparently, Housman only settled on this word having rejected: vex, plague, tear, wrench rend, wring, break and pierce (Marlow 140).

Guiding Questions:

1. What contrasts are made by the speaker between the period before he was born and the period after?
2. What was the same about the state of the world before and after his birth? What was the key difference for him?
3. Express in your own words the question to which the speaker can find no

answer. What course of action is recommended?

4. Given the nature of life as he sees it, what is the only thing the speaker looks forward to?

Final Thoughts:

This poem returns to the theme explored in "Wenlock Edge": from the moment an individual is born on Earth, he or she has to experience pain till the moment they die. It is a deeply pessimistic message since human suffering is unredeemed either by divine or human love.

In stanza one, the speaker uses Christian concepts ("my soul … high heaven"), but without the any reference to faith in redemption or to a connection between a person's life on Earth and salvation. Rather, the "soul" (by which he seems to mean 'the mind' or 'the individual being') is seen to be inherently immortal, woken from restful slumber to suffer the grief that is life only to return, inevitably, to the "days when we had rest." There is no point in the soul struggling against the griefs of life, for its weapons are too fragile, while earth and the universe are strong. Note how the sound of line one reinforces this message: the long consonants (the alliterated 's' and the concluding 'l' sounds) contrast with the harder alliteration of the letter 'b' and shorter vowels, particularly in the final word. Instead of fretting about a reality we are powerless to change, he counsels his soul to be calm and remember the "days when we had rest" before birth. Line two stresses the unevenness of the battle. The alliteration of the strong 'h' and 'f' sounds, together with the repeated emphasis in "**fixt of old**" and "**foun**ded **strong**," convey the force of that which is. Those were far longer than is the brief period of his life here on earth, and the soul should find consolation in that.

The speaker continues in stanza two to describe his state while he was "in the quarry"; that is, before his consciousness was formed. The world then was full of "unkindness," "tears," "sweat and blood," but he, lacking consciousness of it, experienced only "lightless." He "slept and saw not" and therefore "did not mourn." The suffering that is life is emphasized in lines six and seven by repetition and listing. This is an interesting variation on the Judeo-Christian myth of the loss of innocence in the Garden of Eden. In both cases, suffering is attributed to man gaining knowledge of good and evil and falling into sin, but in Housman's mythology this is an inevitable process in an indifferent universe, while in *Genesis* it is the punishment by a divine being, "OF Man's First Disobedience, and the Fruit / Of that Forbidden Tree, whose mortal taste / Brought Death into the World, and all our woe" (Milton *Paradise Lost* Book One). The speaker says, "Be still, be still, my soul." The repetition here (with variation) of the opening line, emphasizes how difficult it is for the individual consciousness to achieve patience in the face of life's trials. I also suspect that Housman intends the reader to recall the verses, "Be still, and know that I am God: I will be exalted among the heathen, I will be exalted in the earth. The Lord of hosts is with us; the God of Jacob is our refuge. Selah." (*Psalm* 46.10-11, King James Version). The entire point of the poem is to describe a life absent that transcendent reassurance.

In stanza three the speaker, like many philosophers before him, seeks to understand the meaning of life and its relationship to eternity. Not surprisingly, he admits to never having found an answer. His counsel to his soul is to accept the inexplicable reality that, for the present, he walks the earth, breathes, feels the sun. If existence cannot be explained, it also cannot be denied. Consolation exists only in that our wakening to consciousness is just for "a season." "Let us endure an hour and see injustice done," he tells himself, recommending passivity and acceptance of the cruelties and injustices of life, consoled by the knowledge that it will soon be over.

In the final stanza, the speaker condemns "high heaven and earth" as inherently flawed from their "prime foundation." The use of the word "foundation" rather than 'creation' suggests the universe is as it is by chance rather than by design. Then the speaker really piles on the negatives: human existence is characterized by, "Horror and scorn and hate and fear and indignation," the thought about which tears the heart to shreds – and all to no end. Once again, despite his own injunctions against such speculation, he is forced to ask the question, "Oh why did I awake? When shall I sleep again?" It is, however, an unanswerable question. All he can do is to look forward to the return to unconsciousness that will come with death, so the only valid question is "when shall I sleep again?

XLIX

Think no more, lad; laugh, be jolly:
  Why should men make haste to die?
Empty heads and tongues a-talking
  Make the rough road easy walking,
And the feather pate of folly   5
  Bears the falling sky.

Oh, 'tis jesting, dancing, drinking
  Spins the heavy world around.
If young hearts were not so clever,
  Oh, they would be young for ever: 10
Think no more; 'tis only thinking
  Lays lads underground.

Notes:

"If after the manner of men I have fought with beasts at Ephesus, what advantageth it me, if the dead rise not? let us eat and drink; for to morrow we die" (*1 Corinthians* 15:32 King James Version).

"feather pate" – Presumably an earlier version of the terms "bird-brain" and "scatter-brain" meaning someone who is not terribly bright, is silly or absent-minded.

Guiding Questions:

1. What, according to stanza one, is the best way to get through the "rough road" of life?
2. What, according to stanza two, is the secret of eternal youth?
3. How seriously is the reader supposed to take the prescriptions for living given in the poem? How do you know?

Final Thoughts:

In many ways, this poem is a counterblast to the previous one (a pattern that is common in the collection). Here the theme is that the way to live is to get all the fun one can out of life (the previous poem did not envisage that there *was* any chance for men to "laugh, be jolly") and not to think about dying. The advice the speaker gives is evidently ironic: empty-headed jabbering and bird-brained folly are the best way to get through the "rough road" of life. Anti-intellectualism is the apparent theme, but it is expressed in nonsensical hyperbole. "If young hearts were not so clever, / Oh, they would be young for ever," the speaker says, but the reader understands immediately that this is, at best, wishful thinking, at worse, cruel self-delusion. The 'cure' for consciousness is, he says to, "Think no more"; that is, to cease being human. He concludes with another statement that simply will not survive scrutiny, "'tis only thinking / Lays lads underground." Actually, it is not: disease, wars, accidents, and old age – these are the things that lay lads (whether they are prone to thought or not) underground. The poem, then, is a satire of the views it purports to approvingly express.

L

Clunton and Clunbury,
   Clungunford and Clun,
Are the quietest places
   Under the sun.

In valleys of springs of rivers,   5
   By Ony and Teme and Clun,
The country for easy livers,
   The quietest under the sun,

We still had sorrows to lighten,
   One could not be always glad,   10
And lads knew trouble at Knighton
   When I was a Knighton lad.

By bridges that Thames runs under,
   In London, the town built ill,
'Tis sure small matter for wonder   15
   If sorrow is with one still.

And if as a lad grows older
   The troubles he bears are more,
He carries his griefs on a shoulder
   That handselled them long before.   20

Where shall one halt to deliver
   This luggage I'd lief set down?
Not Thames, not Teme is the river,
   Nor London nor Knighton the town:

'Tis a long way further than Knighton,   25
   A quieter place than Clun,
Where doomsday may thunder and lighten
   And little 'will matter to one.

Notes:

I recommend consulting the *Telegraph* Travel article, "Walk of the month: Christopher Somerville finds that tranquility reigns still in the Shropshire villages immortalised by AE Housman." Just search for it on-line.
"Clunton"- A village in south-west Shropshire.

"Clunbury" – A village in south Shropshire.

"Clungunford" – A village in south Shropshire.

"Clun" – A small town in south Shropshire on the River Clun which rises near the Wales/England border and flows into the River Teme in Herefordshire.

"Ony" – The River Onny flows from the hamlet of Eaton to the River Teme.

"Teme" – A river that rises in mid-Wales and flows through Knighton and down to Ludlow in Shropshire.

"Thames" – A river that rises in the Cotswold Hills and flows roughly due west through Oxford and London.

"Knighton" – A small market town in central Powys, Wales. Offa's Dyke, once the border between England and Wales, runs north to south just to the east of the town.

"handselled" – This is the simple past tense and past participle of 'handsel' meaning 'payment.' The idea is that the shoulders paid the price of the burden of suffering even in the quiet land before coming to London.

"lief" – i.e. rather, prefer to.

Guiding Questions:

1. What use does Housman make of place names in the poem?
2. Why are the troubles felt in Shropshire felt even more intensely in London?
3. Where does a person finally get to put down his burden of troubles?

Final Thoughts:

Housman actually knew little of Clunton and Clunbury, Clungunford and Clun, except the most important thing which is that together they sound magical (in the same way that the places in Tolkien's Middle Earth sound magical). The names create a blessed land, the "quietest under the sun" and therefore a "country for easy livers." Yet even here "sorrows ... [and] troubles" cannot be entirely avoided and have to be dealt with.

In London, the speaker still feels "sorrow." Indeed, the "troubles he bears are more," which the speaker attributes to London being a "town built ill." Yet still trouble is a burden ("luggage") that the speaker cannot put down, whether he is in Shropshire or London. Troubles will only be "set down" in death because then one will not feel trouble – or anything else. The pun on the penultimate line embodies the paradoxical meaning of the poem. Doomsday will both strike with the destructive terror of lightning and relieve the load of man's suffering.

LI

    Loitering with a vacant eye
Along the Grecian gallery,
And brooding on my heavy ill,
I met a statue standing still.
Still in marble stone stood he,   5
And stedfastly he looked at me.
"Well met," I thought the look would say,
"We both were fashioned far away;
We neither knew, when we were young,
These Londoners we live among."   10

    Still he stood and eyed me hard,
An earnest and a grave regard:
"What, lad, drooping with your lot?
I too would be where I am not.
I too survey that endless line   15
Of men whose thoughts are not as mine.
Years, ere you stood up from rest,
On my neck the collar prest;
Years, when you lay down your ill,
I shall stand and bear it still.   20
Courage, lad, 'tis not for long:
Stand, quit you like stone, be strong."
So I thought his look would say;
And light on me my trouble lay,
And I slept out in flesh and bone   25
Manful like the man of stone.

Notes:

"Grecian gallery" – i.e., the Department of Greece and Rome at the British Museum.
"prest" – i.e., pressed.
"quit" – i.e., acquit, conduct oneself.

Guiding Questions:

1. What is the speaker's mood as he looks around the Grecian gallery?
2. Make a list of the ways in which the poem compares the experiences of the speaker and the statue.
3. Make a list of the ways in which the poem contrasts the experiences of the speaker and the statue.

4. What is the message that the statue passes onto the speaker? Does it help? Why or why not?

Final Thoughts:

Stanza one begins with movement and action ("Loitering ... Along ... brooding") but comes to an abrupt halt on line four. This is achieved by a combination of short vowels, the 's' alliteration (in this context, unusually, a short sound) and the heavy end-stop punctuation. Line five virtually repeats the same techniques to create the same effect – the speaker's motion has been stopped. The contrast is established then between the speaker and the statue, which seems to exude an almost supernatural calm. The speaker, however, imagines the statue pointing to an essential similarity between them, "We both were fashioned far away" – one in Greece and one in Shropshire.

Stanza two expands on the similarities. The statue says (or appears to say) that he also "would be where I am not," and that he also sees an "endless line / Of men whose thoughts are not as mine." They are both surrounded by strangers. Yet the statue points out that on his "neck the collar prest" centuries before the speaker became conscious of feeling it oppress him and that when the speaker lays down his burden (by dying) he will, "shall stand and bear it still." The collar may be literally a slave's collar, but more likely the slave's collar is an effective metaphor for enslavement to the human condition. So, from the Greek statue the speaker learns stoicism: to live in harmony with one's fate, to be indifferent to the vicissitudes of fortune, and to treat pleasure and pain alike. The statue's message is, "quit you like stone" – and the speaker does.

LII

Far in a western brookland
    That bred me long ago
The poplars stand and tremble
    By pools I used to know.

There, in the windless night-time,   5
    The wanderer, marvelling why,
Halts on the bridge to hearken
    How soft the poplars sigh.

He hears: long since forgotten
    In fields where I was known,   10
Here I lie down in London
    And turn to rest alone.

There, by the starlit fences,
    The wanderer halts and hears
My soul that lingers sighing   15
    About the glimmering weirs.

Notes:

"brookland" – i.e., the land of small streams.

"weirs" – A weir is a low dam designed to raise the level of the water flowing down a river. When the water is raised to the required height, the water then flows over the top of the weir.

Guiding Questions:

1. In what ways does the speaker personify the "western brookland" where he was raised?
2. Who has taken the speaker's place there?
3. Little is said about London. What impression do you gain of it from lines 11 and 12?
4. What exactly does the wanderer hear in the last stanza? What does that imply about the speaker?

Final Thoughts:

The speaker is wistfully reminiscent of his early years. He longingly recalls the pastoral beauties of his homeland: its brooks, its poplars and its pools. He laments the loss of a place, a time, and a condition of innocence and happiness.

Not only was he there surrounded by nature: he was born and raised by nature which is personified. The "western brookland / ... bred [him]," the "poplars stand and tremble," and the pools "used to know [him]." This was a living landscape.

The speaker's sense of loss is heightened by his awareness that the golden land continues to be beautiful even though he is cut off from its beauties. He feels that he has been "long since forgotten" be the land that he remembers so well. Now, others stop, as he once did, "to hearken / How soft the poplars sigh." He imagines, at this very moment, a wanderer communing with nature.

London symbolizes the loss of innocence that comes with age. It is not described at all, "Here I lie down in London / And turn to rest alone." Notice the alliteration of the 'l' sound which gives such a dead feel to these lines. London is a place of toil (hence the need to rest) and isolation (something of a paradox in a city) and resulting loneliness. It does not offer a. sense of oneness either with nature or human community.

Not only is he alienated from his own country, but he describes himself as a ghost haunting the places he loves. He is there still, "sighing" for his loss. London is the dead land.

LIII   THE TRUE LOVER

The lad came to the door at night,
    When lovers crown their vows,
And whistled soft and out of sight
    In shadow of the boughs.

"I shall not vex you with my face   5
    Henceforth, my love, for aye;
So take me in your arms a space
    Before the east is grey."

"When I from hence away am past
    I shall not find a bride,   10
And you shall be the first and last
    I ever lay beside."

She heard and went and knew not why;
    Her heart to his she laid;
Light was the air beneath the sky   15
    But dark under the shade.

"Oh do you breathe, lad, that your breast
    Seems not to rise and fall,
And here upon my bosom prest
    There beats no heart at all?"   20

"Oh loud, my girl, it once would knock,
    You should have felt it then;
But since for you I stopped the clock
    It never goes again."

"Oh lad, what is it, lad, that drips   25
    Wet from your neck on mine?
What is it falling on my lips,
    My lad, that tastes of brine?"

"Oh like enough 'tis blood, my dear,
    For when the knife has slit   30
The throat across from ear to ear
    'Twill bleed because of it."

Under the stars the air was light
  But dark below the boughs,
The still air of the speechless night,   35
  When lovers crown their vows.

Notes:

"prest" – i.e., pressed.

Guiding Questions:

1. Describe the setting of the poem: where, when, who?
2. The man wants the woman to let him in so that they can make love. What three arguments does he make to persuade her to allow him to do that?
3. Why does she let him in? What happens?

Final Thoughts:

This story of a lover's tryst at night is the stuff of traditional romantic ballads, as is the dramatic turning point in the relationship and the melodramatic violence of the story. The woman is the faithless one; the man is the "True Lover" of the title who has given her his heart. Whether the woman once seemed to respond and has changed her mind or was always indifferent to his feelings is not clear. Certainly, the man is now aware that his love is hopeless, but he comes to beg of her one night of sexual consummation. He assures her that he will not "'vex'" her with his face (it is dark remember), promises her that he will leave the area, "When I from hence away am past." Both the woman and the reader probably miss the pun on the word "past." Initially it seems to mean only 'far away,' but 'to pass' is a euphemism for 'to die.' He promises to be true to their one night of love, "'you shall be the first and last / I ever lay beside.'" The full import of this statement is also only evident later in the poem. Convinced of the transitory nature of human love, the speaker has concluded that only by death can man free himself from the inconstancy that rules his life: the true lover is the one who commits suicide at the moment of love's consummation (one might almost say of orgasm) in the full awareness that love will never be so wonderful again.

It works, for she lets him in and, "Her heart to his she laid." This seems to indicate some softening, some awareness of the suffering she has caused. However, her uncomprehending question, "'Oh do you breathe[?]'" suggests that she entirely lacks empathy. The heartless beloved is punished in the most gruesome way for her lack of feeling and the description leaves little to the imagination: the true lover slits his throat in the dark, and his blood falls on her lips. There is a fine irony about the last two lines, "'And here upon my bosom prest / There beats no heart at all?'" The point of the poem is that it is the woman who is heartless not the man.

LIV

> With rue my heart is laden
> For golden friends I had,
> For many a rose-lipt maiden
> And many a lightfoot lad.
>
> By brooks too broad for leaping   5
> The lightfoot boys are laid;
> The rose-lipt girls are sleeping
> In fields where roses fade.

Notes:

Read "Nothing Gold Can Stay" (1923) Robert Frost (1874-1963). It has a similar theme and use of gold.

Go to YouTube and search for the song, "Who Knows Where the Time Goes" by Sandy Denny. It is hauntingly beautiful – particularly given the premature death of the singer.

"rue" – i.e., bitter regret. Rue (also called 'herb-of-grace') is an herb and ornamental plant symbolic of regret. It is one of the flowers distributed by the mad Ophelia in Shakespeare's *Hamlet*: "There's fennel for you, and columbines. – There's rue for you, and here's some for me. We may call it 'herb of grace' o' Sundays. – Oh, you must wear your rue with a difference" (Act 4 Scene 5). Rue stands in contrast to the rose in the poem.

"lipt" – i.e. lipped.

"rose-lipt" – Red roses symbolize love and romance. The term 'rosebud mouth' (or lips) describes a woman's mouth or lips that have a round shape like the petals of a rose and are very red. They are generally seen to be attractive – well, sexy to be honest.

Guiding Questions:

1. How are the lasses and lads whom the speaker once knew idealized?
2. What might the broad brooks and fading roses symbolize?

Final Thoughts:

This is a perfect little poem that, in its simplicity, almost seems to need no analysis … almost. In fact, it is carefully crafted. The speaker is not concerned with a specific death but with the phenomenon of death itself. The first line sets the melancholy tone and the repetition of the word "many" shows that his sorrow is cumulative. Regret is presented in a metaphor as a physical burden on the heart, and that regret undercuts the idealized picture that the speaker conjures up of the lads and lasses he knew as a youth. The red lips of the girls are compared in another metaphor with the red blossom of roses, and the fleetness of foot of the boys becomes an adjective that totally defines them. The emphasis in line four falls on the 'l' alliteration, giving the words the rhythm of jumping feet. We already know, however, that the lads are dead.

In stanza two, the broad brooks symbolize mortality – one cannot but think of the River Styx which in Greek mythology was the river that formed the boundary between Earth and the Underworld (Hades). For all their athleticism, the lads could not transcend their mortality. The fading roses symbolize the inevitability of aging and death. The beautiful young lasses were caught in the natural cycle of generation, birth and aging, until they escape it in death. The rhyming of "laid" and "fade" is particularly effective as it places stress on the common fate of the lads and lasses.

LV

Westward on the high-hilled plains
    Where for me the world began,
Still, I think, in newer veins
    Frets the changeless blood of man.

Now that other lads than I   5
    Strip to bathe on Severn shore,
They, no help, for all they try,
    Tread the mill I trod before.

There, when hueless is the west
    And the darkness hushes wide,   10
Where the lad lies down to rest
    Stands the troubled dream beside.

There, on thoughts that once were mine,
    Day looks down the eastern steep,
And the youth at morning shine   15
    Makes the vow he will not keep.

Notes:

"Tread the mill" – A treadmill was a machine used to power other machines (such as those designed to raise water or to grind grain). It consisted of a large wheel with steps fitted and was turned by the weight of people treading the steps. This was a boring but also an exhausting and endless job – for which reason slaves and convicts were often enforced to do it.
"no help" – i.e., no avoiding it.
"hueless" – i.e., colorless (it is night).
"steep" – i.e., mountain or hill slope.

Guiding Questions:

1. What is changeless and what subject to change on "the high-hilled plains"?
2. With what is life compared in stanza two? What point is the speaker making by this metaphor?
3. Explain the personification in stanza three.
4. Explain the personification in stanza four.

Final Thoughts:

The theme of the first stanza is that of "Wenlock Edge": individual humans change, blood runs in "newer veins," but the blood itself is "changeless," since humanity is timeless. Timeless too, since it comes of being human, is fret about life. In stanza two a metaphor is used comparing living to working on a treadmill like a convict – "for all the try" there is no escape. Notice the importance of alliteration:

> Strip to bathe on Severn shore,
> They, no help, for all they try,
> Tread the mill I trod before.

In line six, the 's' sound produces a vigorous rhythm appropriate to the youthful activity described. In lines seven and eight, however, the heavy 't' alliteration deadens the rhythm suggesting the repetitive action in which the youths are trapped.

In stanza three, worry is personified as standing over the lad when he lies down to go to sleep at night, and in stanza four it looks down on the waking lad who, the speaker knows from his own experience, "Makes the vow he will not keep."

LVI THE DAY OF BATTLE

"Far I hear the bugle blow
To call me where I would not go,
And the guns begin the song,
'Soldier, fly or stay for long.'"

"Comrade, if to turn and fly   5
Made a soldier never die,
Fly I would, for who would not?
'Tis sure no pleasure to be shot."

"But since the man that runs away
Lives to die another day,   10
And cowards' funerals, when they come
Are not wept so well at home."

"Therefore, though the best is bad,
Stand and do the best my lad;
Stand and fight and see your slain,   15
And take the bullet in your brain."

Notes:

Read "The Soldier" (1915) by Rupert Brook (1887-1915) and "An Irish Airman Foresees His Death" (1919)
W. B. Yeats (1865-1939).
Consider the statement by Julius Caesar, "Cowards die many times before their deaths; / The valiant never taste of death but once" (Shakespeare *Julius Caesar* Act 2 Scene 2).

Guiding Questions:

1. What is the significance of the bugle call that opens the poem?
2. What binary choice does each individual soldier face?
3. In stanza two, what does the second speaker say about whether the soldier should fight or run?
4. What two arguments does the second speaker use in stanza three for staying and fighting?
5. Why is the best "bad"? Why should the soldier do it anyway?

Final Thoughts:

This poem is about the eternal dilemma of the frontline soldier: when the advance is called, does he step toward death or run away and save his life? The first voice we hear is that of one such soldier. Stanza one uses the metaphor of music to describe the call to advance, "the **b**ugle **b**low[s] … the guns **b**egin the song.'" Notice the alliteration of the hard 'b' sound that makes the call to battle strong. There is a marked contrast between the connotation of these words and the reality, which is that the soldier is called somewhere he "'would not go,'" somewhere that, if he does go, he is likely to "'stay for long'" (a euphemism for 'die').

Stanza two introduces a second voice, that of a fellow soldier, perhaps the man's sergeant, who comments on what the first has said and puts it into context as only a veteran can. He seems to agree that running away is preferable since, with comic understatement, he points out, "''Tis sure no pleasure to be shot.'" However, the key word "'if'" on line five qualifies his agreement. Only if running away would, "'Made a soldier never die,'" would he advise running away. The truth, however, is that if you run away today, you will only live "'to die another day,'" and when you die then you will be known as a coward and "'not wept so well at home.'"

The final stanza wraps up the second speaker's argument for obeying the call to attack. There are two choices (stay or run), and "'the **b**est is **b**ad'" (notice again the pairing of the forceful 'b' alliteration) because it is likely to get you killed. Nevertheless, the speaker exhorts his comrade to, "'Stand and do the best'"; that is, "'fight and see your slain,'" and be killed, "'take the bullet in your brain.'"

The ostensible message of the poem is clear: be a man; fight, kill and die for your country. The second speaker, whose advice this is, gets twelve lines to the soldier's four and also gets the last, unanswered word. But the poem is a dialogue and the voice of the poet is nowhere present. Does he endorse the views of the second speaker? Housman's respect for soldiers fighting for Queen and Country suggests that he does, but if he was remembering the death of his brother, Herbert Housman, aged 33, fighting in the Boer War in South Africa, then perhaps not. If we look to the text, we find that Housman uses the opposition of "Stand" and fall, "**B**ullet in your **b**rain." The glibness of the advice in the final stanza and the sheer brutality of that last line, emphasized by the hard 'b' alliteration, suggest that the poet is distancing himself from the second speaker's message.

LVII

You smile upon your friend to-day,
   To-day his ills are over;
You hearken to the lover's say,
   And happy is the lover.

'Tis late to hearken, late to smile,   5
   But better late than never:
I shall have lived a little while
   Before I die for ever.

Guiding Questions:

1. The poem is addressed by the speaker to a "friend." Explain why the speaker confides to this friend that "his ills are over."
2. What is the speaker's friend doing for the first time in their relationship? How does the speaker react?
3. Is the person being addressed male or female?

Final Thoughts:

The poem is directly addressed to a lover, acknowledging that this person is now, finally, listening to him speak of his love. That this openness to his love is "better late than never" is true, but little consolation since it *is* too late, except that the speaker will have lived a little before death takes him forever.

Line two, "To-day his ills are over," is deliberately ambiguous. At first it seems that the speaker's ills are over because his friend is, for the first time apparently, listening to his declaration of love, but later in the poem it becomes clear that the speaker's ills are over because he has abandoned any hope of having his affections returned and is determined to die.

LVIII

When I came last to Ludlow
  Amidst the moonlight pale,
Two friends kept step beside me,
  Two honest lads and hale.

Now Dick lies long in the churchyard,   5
  And Ned lies long in jail,
And I come home to Ludlow
  Amidst the moonlight pale.

Guiding Questions:

1. Describe the tone of stanza one. What are the key words that create that tone?
2. How does the speaker make the fates of Dick and Ned shocking to the reader?
3. What significance do you find in the "moonlight"?

Final Thoughts:

Stanza one appears to be very positive. The alliteration of the 'l' sound gives line one the confident rhythm of a striding man. That the two friends "kept step" with the speaker implies a unity between them, and the adjectives "honest" and "hale," emphasized by the use of alliteration, establish their moral and physical health. Only the "moonlight pale" even suggests an ominous note. While sunlight has only positive connotations, "moonlight" inevitably carries negative associations of mystery, evil, and even madness.

The contrast between lines four and five is stark. Line five is the longest line in the poem in terms of syllables (eight). It is also lengthened by the 'l' alliteration and long vowels, "Lies long." Line six is by contrast much shorter containing six monosyllables. The long 'l' sounds and vowels occur here too, but they are bracketed by short 'a' and 'e' vowels. Both lines convey finality. The repetition of the opening lines, with the important change of tense, bring the poem full circle, but this only serves to emphasis how much has changed since "last [he came] to Ludlow."

LIX   THE ISLE OF PORTLAND

The star-filled seas are smooth to-night
   From France to England strown;
Black towers above the Portland light
   The felon-quarried stone.

On yonder island, not to rise,   5
   Never to stir forth free,
Far from his folk a dead lad lies
   That once was friends with me.

Lie you easy, dream you light,
   And sleep you fast for aye;   10
And luckier may you find the night
   Than ever you found the day.

Notes:

"Portland" – The Isle of Portland (4 miles long by 1.7 miles wide) lies in the English Channel some two miles south of Weymouth in Dorset. In fact, it is not a true island since it is connected to the mainland by a barrier beach called Chesil Beach. Its main claim to fame is the fine limestone that is quarried there.
"strown" – i.e., strewn.
"Portland light" – Portland Bill, the southern tip of the island of Portland, had two lighthouses at this time: The Higher Lighthouse and the Lower Lighthouse. A third was built in 1906 which replaced them.
"felon-quarried" – HM Prison Portland in the village of The Grove on Portland was opened in 1848.

Guiding Questions:

1. Where do you imagine the speaker to be in stanza one? Why?
2. How is the mood of the first two lines different from that of the second two? What creates the different moods?
3. What details in stanza two make the reader feel sympathetic with the dead man?
4. What does the speaker wish his friend?

Final Thoughts:

The first two lines sound idyllic. The calm sea reflects the stars. Note the use of superlatives: the sea is "star-filled," for stars are "strown" across its surface – the alliteration of the sibilant 's' sound adding to the calm mood. Then things change. Oxymoronically, the "Portland light" rises "black" against the night, and the speaker reminds us that it is built of "felon-quarried stone." Death and incarceration are suggested.

In stanza two, it immediately becomes clear that the speaker (and therefore the reader) is not actually on Portland Island, but looking across a gulf toward it. Note the alliteration of the harsh, short 'f' and 'l' sounds in the description of the dead friend. The line, "Never to stir forth free," identifies him as a convict who has died in prison; he lies in the prison grave yard separated from "his folk ... [who] once was friend with me." The 'f' alliteration unifies the description of the dead man in this stanza.

The final stanza uses the common trope (i.e., any figure of speech through which writers intend to express meanings of words differently than their literal meanings) of death as sleep. The speaker hopes that his friend will enjoy in death the "easy ... light ... sleep" that he was denied in life and that his night of death will be "luckier" than his life of day ever was. The final impression of the poem is of the unfairness of life.

LX

> Now hollow fires burn out to black,
>> And lights are guttering low:
> Square your shoulders, lift your pack,
>> And leave your friends and go.
>
> Oh never fear, man, nought's to dread,   5
>> Look not left nor right:
> In all the endless road you tread
>> There's nothing but the night,

Notes:

"pack" – The word has military connotations.

Guiding Questions:

1. Who is the speaker and whom is the person being addressed?
2. In your own words explain the reasons why the lad should leave his "friends and go."

Final Thoughts:

The theme of the first two lines is entropy (i.e., gradual decline into disorder). The purposeful fires and lights are burning themselves "out to black … are guttering low." Life seems to be shrinking into inertia. In contrast, we then get the imperative verbs of the next two lines ("Square … lift … leave"). The long vowels of the first two lines are replaced by short, hard vowels and the abrupt, paired alliteration of the 's' and 'l' sounds:

> Square your shoulders, lift your pack,
> And leave your friends and go.

The lines are a call to action, a call not to let life drift away.

The second stanza addresses the potential recruit's fear that going for a soldier will result in his death. The speaker, who sounds at this point like a cajoling sergeant, reassures the man that there is nothing to fear and "nought's to dread" because:

> In all the endless road you tread
> There's nothing but the night.

The sergeant means to be reassuring. However, his ultimate reason, given in the final two lines, is shocking: the only end of life is death ("nothing but the night"). Note the thumping certainty of the 'n' alliteration.

LXI   *HUGHLEY STEEPLE*

The vane on Hughley steeple
   Veers bright, a far-known sign,
And there lie Hughley people,
   And there lie friends of mine.
Tall in their midst the tower   5
   Divides the shade and sun,
And the clock strikes the hour
   And tells the time to none.

To south the headstones cluster,
   The sunny mounds lie thick;   10
The dead are more in muster
   At Hughley than the quick.
North, for a soon-told number,
   Chill graves the sexton delves,
And steeple-shadowed slumber   15
   The slayers of themselves.

To north, to south, lie parted,
   With Hughley tower above,
The kind, the single-hearted,
   The lads I used to love.   20
And, south or north, 'tis only
   A choice of friends one knows,
And I shall ne'er be lonely
   Asleep with these or those.

Notes:

"Hughley steeple" – Hughley is a village in mid-Shropshire about a mile north-west of Wenlock Edge. The Church of St John the Baptist dates back to the thirteenth and fourteenth century. The timber-framed bell tower was built about 1700. It is short, so effectively the church does not have a steeple. There is, however, a tall weather cock on top.

"muster" – i.e. to assemble – particularly of troops for inspection or preparation for battle.

"the quick" – i.e., the living.

"told" – i.e., counted.

"sexton" – i.e., grave digger.

"delves" – i.e., digs. Compare, "When Adam delved and Eve span, / Who was then the gentleman?" (John Ball [c.1338-1381] English priest prominent in the

Study Guide

Peasants' Revolt of 1381).

"slayers of themselves" – "Up until the 19th century the Church [of England] refused to offer Christian funerals for people who had committed suicide with a 'sound mind' or for those who hadn't been baptised. This was updated in the 1880s to permit priests to bury those who had taken their own life but without the standard service set out in the Anglican Book of Common Prayer." This reflected the traditional Church position that suicide is a sin. Although it had long been ignored, the ban on full Christian funerals for people who commit suicide was only lifted in 2017. (Adeogun, Eno. "Church ends ban on full Christian funerals for suicides." *Premier*. 11 Jul. 2017. Web. 8 Oct. 2019.)

Guiding Questions:

1. Comment on the contrast between the vertical spire and the horizontal dead.
2. What distinction is made between two types of graves in the churchyard?
3. In the final stanza, what does the speaker say unites the dead in the churchyard and himself?

Final Thoughts:

The contrast in stanza one is between the vertical steeple ("far known ... Tall") and the horizontal dead ("lie ... lie"), and between the existence of the church steeple within time and of the dead out of time ("the clock strikes the hour / And tells the time to none"). The contrast in stanza two is between the numerous graves in the churchyard and the sparse population of the village ("The dead are more in muster / At Hughley than the quick"). A further distinction is made between those who received a full Christian burial, whose south-facing "sunny mounds lie thick," and the smaller number of suicides, their number soon told, who lie in "Chill graves" on the north of the graveyard. The latter fall under the shadow of the steeple (symbolizing the Church's condemnation of their sin).

The final stanza destroys the binary distinctions of the first two stanzas. Both sets who "lie parted" by the church (literally by the tower) are, the speaker tells us, "lads I used to love"; they are all, "The kind, the single-hearted." There is really no distinction between them; it is "only / A choice of friends one knows." Nor is the distinction between the quick and the dead as absolute as it appeared to be, for the speaker tells us, "I shall ne'er be lonely / Asleep with these or those."

LXII

"Terence, this is stupid stuff:
You eat your victuals fast enough;
There can't be much amiss, 'tis clear,
To see the rate you drink your beer.
But oh, good Lord, the verse you make,   5
It gives a chap the belly-ache.
The cow, the old cow, she is dead;
It sleeps well, the horned head:
We poor lads, 'tis our turn now
To hear such tunes as killed the cow.   10
Pretty friendship 'tis to rhyme
Your friends to death before their time
Moping melancholy mad:
Come, pipe a tune to dance to, lad."

Why, if 'tis dancing you would be,   15
There's brisker pipes than poetry.
Say, for what were hop-yards meant,
Or why was Burton built on Trent?
Oh many a peer of England brews
Livelier liquor than the Muse,   20
And malt does more than Milton can
To justify God's ways to man.
Ale, man, ale's the stuff to drink
For fellows whom it hurts to think:
Look into the pewter pot   25
To see the world as the world's not.
And faith, 'tis pleasant till 'tis past:
The mischief is that 'twill not last.
Oh I have been to Ludlow fair
And left my necktie God knows where,   30
And carried half-way home, or near,
Pints and quarts of Ludlow beer:
Then the world seemed none so bad,
And I myself a sterling lad;
And down in lovely muck I've lain,   35
Happy till I woke again.
Then I saw the morning sky:
Heigho, the tale was all a lie;
The world, it was the old world yet,
I was I, my things were wet,   40

And nothing now remained to do
But begin the game anew.

    Therefore, since the world has still
Much good, but much less good than ill,
And while the sun and moon endure   45
Luck's a chance, but trouble's sure,
I'd face it as a wise man would,
And train for ill and not for good.
'Tis true the stuff I bring for sale
Is not so brisk a brew as ale: 50
Out of a stem that scored the hand
I wrung it in a weary land.
But take it: if the smack is sour,
The better for the embittered hour;
It should do good to heart and head   55
When your soul is in my soul's stead;
And I will friend you, if I may,
In the dark and cloudy day.

    There was a king reigned in the East:
There, when kings will sit to feast,   60
They get their fill before they think
With poisoned meat and poisoned drink.
He gathered all that springs to birth
From the many-venomed earth;
First a little, thence to more,   65
He sampled all her killing store;
And easy, smiling, seasoned sound,
Sate the king when healths went round.
They put arsenic in his meat
And stared aghast to watch him eat;   70
They poured strychnine in his cup
And shook to see him drink it up:
They shook, they stared as white's their shirt:
Them it was their poison hurt.
– I tell the tale that I heard told.   75
Mithridates, he died old.

Notes:

"victuals" – i.e., food.
"The cow, the old cow, she is dead" – This is a reference to the idiom, "The tune

the old cow died of," which refers to advice or complaints being given in the place of actual help or assistance to change a bad situation. The phrase refers to an old song about a farmer who serenaded his cow about the lack of grass, instead of feeding her:

> There was an old man and he had an old cow,
> But he had no fodder to give her,
> So he took up his fiddle and played her the tune:
> "Consider, good cow, consider,
> This isn't the time for the grass to grow,
> Consider, good cow, consider."

"moping melancholy mad": This is a deliberate near-quotation from Book XI of John Milton's epic poem *Paradise Lost*. The words, "moping melancholy / And moon-struck madness," appear in a list of diseases fatal to man spoken to Adam by the Angel Michael. This marks Adam's anguished discovery of human mortality.

"hop-yards" – Hops are an essential ingredient in beer.

"Burton built on Trent" – Burton-on-Trent is a market town in Staffordshire noted for centuries for the brewing of good beer.

"peer" – i.e., nobleman, lord.

"the Muse" – Actually there were nine Muses, the ancient Greek goddesses of science and art, of whom four were believed to inspire the creation of poetry. The poetic muse this means the inspiration to write poetry.

"Milton" – John Milton (1608-1674) was an English poet and thinker. Book One of his epic poem *Paradise Lost* (1658 to 1664) states, "I may assert eternal providence, / And justify the ways of God to men." Milton's theme is the cause and consequences of man's fall in the Garden of Eden. His stated aim is to "justify" the short, harsh life of man as God's punishment for Original Sin.

"venomed" – i.e., containing many poisons.

"healths" – i.e., toasts.

"Mithridates" – Mithridates VI "is said to have lived in the wilderness for seven years, inuring himself to hardship. While there, and after his accession, he cultivated an immunity to poisons by regularly ingesting sub-lethal doses of the same. He invented a complex 'universal antidote' against poisoning..." (Wikipedia contributors. "Mithridates VI of Pontus." *Wikipedia, The Free Encyclopedia*. Wikipedia, The Free Encyclopedia, 2 Oct. 2019. Web. 8 Oct. 2019.)

Guiding Questions:

1. In stanza one: Who is the speaker? To whom is he speaking? What is the main point he is making? What sort of relationship do the two men seem to have? What impression do you get about the speaker's tone?

2. Who is the speaker in the rest of the poem? Why does the poet not use speech

marks?

3. In stanza two, what effects of getting drunk (or at least tipsy) are described? What exactly is the second speaker's point in telling the tale of the time he got drunk at Ludlow fair and what happened as a result?

4. Describe the difference in tone between stanzas two and three. (Remember, it is the same speaker.)

5. In stanza three, the speaker admits that his poems are not wildly popular. Where does he make this concession? Why do you think he is accepting the other person's criticism? What does he argue to be the value of his poems?

6. Stanza four tells the story of King Mithridates. What analogy does the speaker make between what the king did to keep himself alive and the efficacy of the kind of poems that he writes? Is this a convincing argument to you?

Final Thoughts:

Leggett writes that, in this poem, Housman focuses on one aspect of his own poetry:

> the despondent and pessimistic nature of his verse, [and] its painful effect on the reader. The general aesthetic issue which Housman considers in "Terence" is one that has interested theorists since Aristotle. Simply stated, it is this: how can an art that deals with the unpleasant and the painful, bring pleasure, or some corresponding benefit, to its audience? (*Poetic Art* 114).

The poem is a dialogue between Terence, the persona who is the voice of (most of) the poems in the collection and is ostensibly the author of them all, and a friend who has read them. The latter is given the first fourteen lines to state his objections to Terence's poems, and Terrence claims the remaining sixty-two lines to present a model of poetry that justifies the pain and anxiety generated in the reader.

In the first stanza, the friend initially complains to Terence about him writing poetry that is somber and thought-provoking rather than uplifting and celebratory. The first line is shockingly colloquial and made extra forceful by the 's' alliteration and the shortness of the line (it is seven syllables not eight: "'**TERENCE, this** is **stupid stuff**'"). Line two settles into regular iambic tetrameter, which is the basic meter for this poem: "'You **eat** your **vic**tuals **fast enough.**'" The speaker mocks Terence's heartily unpoetic eating and drinking habits, pointing to a comic disparity between the sour verse that he writes that "'gives a chap the belly-ache,'" and his own healthy appetite, eating his "'victuals fast enough'" and quickly downing his beer. From this evidence, he concludes, "'There can't be much amiss, 'tis clear,'" which carries the implication that the sadness and melancholy of the poetry must be fake. The expletive, the mildly profane, "'oh, good Lord'" suggest that the speaker is teasing his friend rather than making a serious complaint.

Lines 7-8 are a parody of the sort of "'silly stuff'" the speaker is complaining about in the form of a pathetic poem about the death of a cow. Not only is the parody very funny (and remarkably accurate in terms of the style of the poems in this collection), the speaker adds the joke that it was "'tunes'" (verses) like Terence's that killed the cow. Similarly, he adds, Terence is in danger of rhyming his "'friends to death before their time.'" This is an example of comic hyperbole, "Terence's poetry is seen as a kind of disease that has infected the poet, 'killed the cow,' and now threatens to send his 'friends to death before their time'" (Leggett *Poetic Art* 117).

Line 13 parodies Terence's love of alliteration offering three negative adjectives that sum up the essence of his poems, "'**M**oping **m**elancholy **m**ad.'" Enough of serious poetry – his friends would prefer something happier, "'a tune to dance to.'" Perhaps Housman is remembering Hamlet's response when Polonious complains about the length of a serious speech: "It shall to the barber's, with your beard. – Prithee, say on. He's for a jig or a tale of bawdry, or he sleeps" (Act 2 Scene 2).

Instead of making all the stanzas the same length, as is normal in Housman's poems, he uses them to help us understand the debate he is depicting and later the different stages of Terence's argument in defense of his poetry. Think of each new stanza as a new paragraph, each with its own subject and tone. Thus, stanza two begins Terence's response. If a person wants to be entertained, "if 'tis dancing you would be," then they should look somewhere else. Keeping up the lighthearted, bantering tone set by his friend, he suggests that beer is a, "Livelier liquor than the Muse." Notice that here he is using precisely that alliteration that his friend earlier mocked. In lines 21-22, he uses comic hyperbole, praising beer ("malt") as better at explaining God's actions to humans than the poet John Milton who set out to do precisely that in his greatest work *Paradise Lost*. Terence's approach to defending poetry in general, and his own poetry in particular, is certainly original: he almost seems to be arguing on his friend's side. Then he hits back, "For fellows whom it hurts to think"; that is, beer is a great way to understand the world, if you are too stupid to think! The problem is that beer, particularly when you have had a lot, shows you "the world as the world's not." Being drunk makes everything seem wonderful, but only for a little while, "The mischief is that 'twill not last." Beer is a temporary pleasure followed by an unpleasant hangover.

Terence recalls his own drunken adventures. One time he got so drunk he lost his tie! Shock horror! Actually, this is a clever use of deliberate bathos by Terence: he creates a trivial or ridiculous anticlimax. The jokes get better. Having drunk a lot at Ludlow Fair, Terence admits that he "carried half way home, or near, / Pints and quarts of Ludlow beer." Cleverly, he leaves it to his friend (and to the reader) to speculate whether the beer came back up or was just urinated away. Terence admits that when drunk, "the world seemed none so bad, / And I myself a sterling lad," but of course that did not last. So happy was he that he lay down in "lovely muck" and went happily to sleep. The phrase "lovely muck" is a well-chosen oxymoron – beer can convince you that even "muck" (which suggests not just mud but mud mixed with animal poo – as in the phrase 'mucking out') is something pleasant. To a drunken man, gross things are beautiful. Waking up sober, it became evident that his alcoholic high "was all a lie"; the world was still the world; he was still himself; and his clothes "were wet." This is another example of deliberate bathos. Terence catches himself on the brink of saying something serious and important about man's relationship with the world, so he stops himself with a comic anti-climax. He concludes despondently, "nothing now remained to do / But begin the game anew." Life seems like a game in that life is meaningless; it is just something you put yourself through. The hard alliteration on the letters 'n' and 'b' add a note of bitterness at the discovery that his drunken vision has been replaced by harsh reality.

Stanza three immediately establishes a more serious tone. The language is still informal, but Terence is now beginning his defense of serious poetry: since life is full of uncertainties, heartbreak, and pain, people should prepare themselves accordingly. "Terence's poetry, in the metaphor of drink that controls the poem, is both painful and sour, but ultimately of more value than attempts to escape the reality of life's ills" (Leggett *Poetic Art* 118). The view of life that emerges is harshly realistic, "the world has still / Much good, but much less good than ill," and "Luck's a chance, but trouble's sure." These statements resemble country aphorisms; they have a folksy tone, but for all that Terence means them – they represent the truth of man's relationship with the world. This being so, wise humans prepare themselves for the worst that can happen, because it probably will. Leggett compares Housman's theory to Sigmund Freud's concept of "'something that seems more primitive, more elementary, more instinctual than the pleasure principle which it over-rides'" (*Ibid.* 120). *In Beyond the Pleasure Principle*, Freud argues that "there is a human need ... a compulsion to defend against the pain of life by deliberately creating anxiety-producing experiences through fantasy or play for the purpose of mastery" (*Ibid.* 121). This is what the critic Lionel Trilling described as "the mithridatic function by which tragedy is used as the homeopathic administration of pain to inure ourselves to the greater pain which life will force upon us" (*Ibid.* 124). If Leggett is right, then by a quarter of a century Housman anticipated Freud's psychoanalytical theory and applied it to the field of aesthetics.

Beginning on line 49, Terence compares beer with his poems. Certainly, beer outsells his poems, he admits with charming self-deprecation. Both beer and poems are squeezed out of grain. In the case of his poems Terence says, "Out of a stem that scored the hand / I wrung it in a weary land." Gone is the comic tone. Terence stresses that his poems come as a result of great effort and at great emotional cost. Notice the harsh verbs, "scored" and "wrung" complemented by the hard vowels and alliteration of the 's' and 'w' letters. Line 53 begins with a firm imperative followed by a mid-line pause (caesura) that gives the reader a moment to let it sink it, "But take it: if the smack is sour, / The better for the embittered hour." If the poetic juice is "sour," it is at lease appropriate since the hour to come is "embittered." It becomes clear that Terence is presenting poetry as an antidote to the miseries of life. When the friend's soul finally comes to the place where Terence's soul is now (and it will), then he will find the poems "should do good to heart and head"; they will be like a friend to support him, "In the dark and cloudy day."

Line 59 begins a detailed analogy that Terence uses to lock down his argument. King Mithridates, knowing himself to be vulnerable to a poisoner, fed himself small quantities of every poison, "From the many-venomed earth," in order to build up his immunity. As a result, he survived every attempt to poison him. Ironically, seeing their failure, his would-be murderers, "Them it was their poison hurt." So that is the use of poetry: trouble is, sooner or later, inevitable, so you should prepare to endure it and sad poems can do that.

LXIII

I hoed and trenched and weeded,
   And took the flowers to fair:
I brought them home unheeded;
   The hue was not the wear.

So up and down I sow them   5
   For lads like me to find,
When I shall lie below them,
   A dead man out of mind.

Some seed the birds devour,
   And some the season mars,   10
But here and there will flower
   The solitary stars,

And fields will yearly bear them
   As light-leaved spring comes on,
And luckless lads will wear them   15
   When I am dead and gone.

Notes

Read "The Wood-Pile" (1912) by Robert Frost (1874-1963). The wood-pile that the speaker discovers may be interpreted as a metaphor for poetry.

"trenched" – i.e., mixed the lower and upper levels of soil

"The hue was not the wear" – i.e., the color was not the fashion.

Stanza three – The thought here is reminiscent of *Matthew* 13: 3-9:

> And he spake many things unto them in parables, saying, Behold, a sower went forth to sow; And when he sowed, some seeds fell by the way side, and the fowls came and devoured them up: Some fell upon stony places, where they had not much earth: and forthwith they sprung up, because they had no deepness of earth: And when the sun was up, they were scorched; and because they had no root, they withered away. And some fell among thorns; and the thorns sprung up, and choked them: But other fell into good ground, and brought forth fruit, some an hundredfold, some sixtyfold, some thirtyfold. Who hath ears to hear, let him hear. (King James Version)

Housman, of course, was quite familiar with the King James Bible. He once remarked, "I think I should describe myself as a High-Church atheist," meaning that he respected the ritual of the national Anglican Church, while not believing its doctrines and dogmas.

Guiding Questions

1. How does the speaker convey his diligence in cultivating flowers?
2. Why did no one buy them?
3. What did he decide to do?
4. What was his hope for his flowers in the future?

Final Thoughts

The speaker has diligently cultivated his flowers: hoeing, trenching and weeding them. He has gathered and taken them to the fair to sell, but found no buyers because they were not the fashionable color to wear. Having brought home his flowers, he decides to take their seeds and sow them "up and down" the countryside where young men will find them after he himself is buried and forgotten. He knows that some of his seeds will be eaten by birds and some ruined by bad weather; only a few seeds will survive to flower like "solitary stars" in the sky. Every spring, these flowers will bloom, and "luckless lads" like the speaker will pluck the blossoms, when the man who originally planted them is "dead and gone."

'Flowers' are a traditional symbol for poetry (e.g., *Les Fleurs du mal* [1857] is a volume of French poetry by Charles Baudelaire [1821-1867]). As the final poem in the cycle, perhaps Housman has in mind his own poems and for once speaks in his own voice – though Housman's poems actually sold very well. Nevertheless, he might have hoped that in future generations a few young men would rediscover them and understand his feelings. The poem explores the paradox that poetry, which is the expression of the writer's awareness of the transience of human life, has the permanence of art; it contains a message of value to man that will withstand the passage of time.

Appendix 1: Extracts from *The Name and Nature of Poetry*

The question should be fairly stated, how far a man can be an adequate, or even a good (so far as he goes) though inadequate critic of poetry, who is not a poet, at least in posse. Can he be an adequate, can he be a good critic, though not commensurate? But there is yet another distinction. Supposing he is not only not a poet, but is a bad poet! What then? (Coleridge, *Anima Poetae,* pp. 127 f.)

THE NAME AND NATURE OF POETRY

...[A]ll my life long the best literature of several languages has been my favourite recreation; and good literature continually read for pleasure must, let us hope, do some good to the reader: must quicken his perception though dull, and sharpen his discrimination though blunt, and mellow the rawness of his personal opinions. But personal opinions they remain, not truths to be imparted as such with the sureness of superior insight and knowledge ...

When one begins to discuss the nature of poetry, the first impediment in the way is the inherent vagueness of the name, and the number of its legitimate senses. It is not bad English to speak of 'prose and poetry' in the sense of 'prose and verse'. But it is wasteful; it squanders a valuable word by stretching it to fit a meaning which is accurately expressed by a wider term. Verse may be, like the Tale of Sir Thomas in the judgment of Our Host of the Tabard, "rym doggerel"; and the name of poetry is generally restricted to verse which can at least be called literature ... There is a conception of poetry which is not fulfilled by pure language and liquid versification, with the simple and so to speak colourless pleasure which they afford, but involves the presence in them of something which moves and touches in a special and recognisable way ... I think that to transfuse emotion – not to transmit thought but to set up in the reader's sense a vibration corresponding to what was felt by the writer – is the peculiar function of poetry ...

There was a whole age of English in which the place of poetry was usurped by something very different which possessed the proper and specific name of wit: wit not in its modern sense, but as defined by Johnson, 'a combination of dissimilar images, or discovery of occult resemblances in things apparently unlike'. Such discoveries are no more poetical than anagrams; such pleasure as they give is purely intellectual and is intellectually frivolous; but this was the pleasure principally sought and found in poems by the intelligentsia of fifty years and more of the seventeenth century. Some of the writers who purveyed it to their contemporaries were, by accident, considerable poets; and though their verse was generally inharmonious, and apparently cut into lengths and tied into faggots by deaf mathematicians, some little of their poetry was beautiful and even superb.

But it was not by this that they captivated and sought to captivate. Simile and metaphor, things inessential to poetry, were their great engrossing pre-occupation, and were prized the more in proportion as they were further fetched. They did not mean these accessories to be helpful, to make their sense clearer or their conceptions more vivid; they hardly even meant them for ornament, or cared whether an image had any independent power to please: their object was to startle by novelty and amuse by ingenuity a public whose one wish was to be so startled and amused ... [P]oetry, as a label for this particular commodity, is not appropriate.

Appropriateness is even more carefully to be considered when the thing which we so much admire that we wish to give it the noblest name we can lay our tongue to is a new thing ... If we apply the word poetry to an object which does not resemble, either in form or content, anything which has heretofore been so called, not only are we maltreating and corrupting language, but we may be guilty of disrespect and blasphemy ...

There is also such a thing as sham poetry, a counterfeit deliberately manufactured and offered as a substitute. In English the great historical example is certain verse produced abundantly and applauded by high and low in what for literary purposes is loosely called the eighteenth century: not a hundred years accidentally begun and ended by chronology, but a longer period which is a unity and a reality; the period lying between *Samson Agonistes* in 1671 and the *Lyrical Ballads* in 1798, and including as an integral part and indeed as its most potent influence the mature work of Dryden ... The writing of poetry proceeded, and much of the poetry written was excellent literature; but excellent literature which is also poetry is not therefore excellent poetry, and the poetry of the eighteenth century was most satisfactory when it did not try to be poetical ... To poets of the eighteenth century high and impassioned poetry did not come spontaneously, because the feelings which foster its birth were not then abundant and urgent in the inner man; but they girt up their loins and essayed a lofty strain at the bidding of ambition. The way to write real poetry, they thought, must be to write something as little like prose as possible; they devised for the purpose what was called a 'correct and splendid diction', which consisted in always using the wrong word instead of the right, and plastered it as ornament, with no thought of propriety, on whatever they desired to dignify. It commanded notice and was not easy to mistake; so the public mind soon connected it with the notion of poetry and came in course of time to regard it as alone poetical.

It was in truth at once pompous and poverty-stricken. It had a very limited, because supposedly choice, vocabulary, and was consequently unequal to the multitude and refinement of its duties. It could not describe natural objects with sensitive fidelity to nature; it could not express human feelings with a variety and delicacy answering to their own. A thick, stiff, unaccommodating medium was interposed between the writer and his work. And this deadening of language had a consequence beyond its own sphere: its effect worked inward, and deadened perception. That which could no longer be described was no longer noticed ...

When I hear anyone say, with defiant emphasis, that Pope was a poet, I suspect him of calling in ambiguity of language to promote confusion of thought ... It is impossible to admire such poetry as Pope's so whole-heartedly as Johnson did, and to rest in it with such perfect contentment, without losing the power to appreciate finer poetry or even to recognise it when met ....

The first impediment, I said, to dealing with the subject of poetry is the native ambiguity of the term. But the course of these remarks has now brought us to a point where another and perhaps greater difficulty awaits us in determining the competence or incompetence of the judge, that is the sensibility or insensibility of the percipient. Am I capable of recognising poetry if I come across it? Do I possess the organ by which poetry is perceived? The majority of civilised mankind notoriously and indisputably do not; who has certified me that I am one of the minority who do? I may know what I like and admire, I may like and admire it intensely; but what makes me think that it is poetry? ... If a man is insensible to poetry, it does not follow that he gets no pleasure from poems. Poems very seldom consist of poetry and nothing else; and pleasure can be derived also from their other ingredients. I am convinced that most readers, when they think that they are admiring poetry, are deceived by inability to analyse their sensations, and that they are really admiring, not the poetry of the passage before them, but something else in it, which they like better than poetry ...

When I examine my mind and try to discern clearly in the matter, I cannot satisfy myself that there are any such things as poetical ideas ... Poetry is not the thing said but a way of saying it ... Meaning is of the intellect, poetry is not. If it were, the eighteenth century would have been able to write it better ... [T]he intellect is not the fount of poetry ... it may actually hinder its production, and ... it cannot even be trusted to recognise poetry when produced ...

Poetry indeed seems to me more physical than intellectual. A year or two ago, in common with others, I received from America a request that I would define poetry. I replied that I could no more define poetry than a terrier can define a rat, but that I thought we both recognised the object by the symptoms which it provokes in us. One of these symptoms was described in connexion with another object by Eliphaz the Temanite: "A spirit passed before my face: the hair of my flesh stood up". Experience has taught me, when I am shaving of a morning, to keep watch over my thoughts, because, if a line of poetry strays into my memory, my skin bristles so that the razor ceases to act. This particular symptom is accompanied by a shiver down the spine; there is another which consists in a constriction of the throat and a precipitation of water to the eyes; and there is a third which I can only describe by borrowing a phrase from one of Keats's last letters, where he says, speaking of Fanny Brawne, "everything that reminds me of her goes through me like a spear". The seat of this sensation is the pit of the stomach.

My opinions on poetry are necessarily tinged, perhaps I should say tainted, by the circumstance that I have come into contact with it on two sides. We were saying a while ago that poetry is a very wide term, and inconveniently comprehensive: so comprehensive is it that it embraces two books, fortunately not large ones, of my own. I know how this stuff came into existence; and though I have no right to assume that any other poetry came into existence in the same way, yet I find reason to believe that some poetry, and quite good poetry, did. Wordsworth for instance says that poetry is the spontaneous overflow of powerful feelings, and Burns has left us this confession, "I have two or three times in my life composed from the wish rather than the impulse, but I never succeeded to any purpose". In short I think that the production of poetry, in its first stage, is less an active than a passive and involuntary process; and if I were obliged, not to define poetry, but to name the class of things to which it belongs, I should call it a secretion; whether a natural secretion, like turpentine in the fir, or a morbid secretion, like the pearl in the oyster. I think that my own case, though I may not deal with the material so cleverly as the oyster does, is the latter; because I have seldom written poetry unless I was rather out of health, and the experience, though pleasurable, was generally agitating and exhausting. If only that you may know what to avoid, I will give some account of the process.

Having drunk a pint of beer at luncheon – beer is a sedative to the brain, and my afternoons are the least intellectual portion of my life – I would go out for a walk of two or three hours. As I went along, thinking of nothing in particular, only looking at things around me and following the progress of the seasons, there would flow into my mind, with sudden and unaccountable emotion, sometimes a line or two of verse, sometimes a whole stanza at once, accompanied, not preceded, by a vague notion of the poem which they were destined to form part of. Then there would usually be a lull of an hour or so, then perhaps the spring would bubble up again. I say bubble up, because, so far as I could make out, the source of the suggestions thus proffered to the brain was an abyss which I have already had occasion to mention, the pit of the stomach. When I got home I wrote them down, leaving gaps, and hoping that further inspiration might be forthcoming another day. Sometimes it was, if I took my walks in a receptive and expectant frame of mind; but sometimes the poem had to be taken in hand and completed by the brain, which was apt to be a matter of trouble and anxiety, involving trial and disappointment, and sometimes ending in failure. I happen to remember distinctly the genesis of the piece which stands last in my first volume. Two of the stanzas, I do not say which, came into my head, just as they are printed, while I was crossing the corner of Hampstead Heath between the Spaniard's Inn and the footpath to Temple Fortune. A third stanza came with a little coaxing after tea. One more was needed, but it did not come: I had to turn to and compose it myself, and that was a laborious business. I wrote it thirteen times, and it was more than a twelvemonth before I got it right ...

Appendix 2: Use of the Study Guide Questions in Reading Groups

Although there are both closed and open questions in this Study Guide, very few of them have simple, answers. They are designed to encourage in-depth discussion, disagreement, thought, further research, and (eventually) consensus. Above all, they aim to encourage readers to go to the text to support their conclusions and interpretations.

I am not so arrogant as to presume to tell you how to use this resource. I used it in the following ways, each of which ensured that students were well prepared for group discussion and presentations. They are described below:

1. Set a reading assignment and tell everyone to be aware that the questions will be the focus of whole group discussion next meeting.

2. Set a reading assignment and allocate particular questions to sections of the group (e.g. if there are four questions, divide the group into four sections, etc.). Form discussion groups containing one person who has prepared each question and allow time for feedback within the groups.
Have feedback to the whole group on each question by picking a group at random to present their answers and to follow up with group discussion.

3. Set a reading assignment, but do not allocate questions. Divide students into groups and allocate to each group one of the questions related to the reading assignment the answer to which they will have to present formally to the group. Allow time for discussion and preparation.

4. Set a reading assignment, but do not allocate questions.
Divide students into groups and allocate to each group one of the questions related to the reading assignment.
Allow time for discussion and preparation. Now reconfigure the groups so that each group contains at least one person who has prepared each question and allow time for feedback within the groups.

5. Before starting to read the text, allocate specific questions to individuals or pairs. (It is best not to allocate all questions to allow for other approaches and variety. One in three questions or one in four seems about right.)
Tell students that they will be leading the group discussion on their question. They will need to start with a brief presentation of the issued and then conduct question and answer. After this, they will be expected to present a brief review

of the discussion.

6. Having finished the text, or part thereof, arrange the group into groups of 3, 4 or 5. Tell each group to select as many questions from the Study Guide as there are members of the group.

Each individual is responsible for drafting out a written answer to one question, and each answer should be a substantial paragraph. Each group as a whole is then responsible for discussing, editing and suggesting improvements to each answer, which is revised by the original writer and brought back to the group for a final proof reading followed by revision.

Appendix 3: Literary Terms

Poetic Terms

Alliteration: when a number of words close together begin with the same first consonant sound (e.g., "Round the rugged rock...") – to understand the contribution of alliteration ask yourself: short or long sounds; soft or harsh sounds; how is the sound of the vowels appropriate to what the words mean?

Assonance: when two or more words repeat the same vowel sound but with different consonant sounds (e.g., "down to the slow, black, sloe-black, crow-black fishing-boat-bobbing sea") – to understand the contribution of assonance ask yourself: short or long sounds; soft or harsh sounds; how is the sound of the vowels appropriate to what the words mean? [Note that, as in the examples above, alliteration and assonance can work together.]

Blank verse: Non-rhyming verse written in iambic pentameter (i.e., each line has ten syllables arranged in pairs: unstressed / stressed).

Caesura: when a break or pause occurs in the middle of a line of verse – the break may be indicated by a punctuation mark or it may be a natural pause.

Couplet: the name for two lines of poetry – they may be rhymed or unrhymed.

Enjambment: when a line of poetry does not end with a pause but 'runs-on' to the next line without a syntactical or rhythmical break – its opposite is an end stopped line which ends with terminal punctuation at the end of a sentence or clause.

Foot / Feet: lines of poetry are divided into units called feet – each foot normally has two syllables and most often these are iambic (unstressed / stressed), but there are other arrangements – it is the pattern of feet that establishes the meter of a poem.

Meter: the pattern of stressed and unstressed syllables in a line or lines of poetry. A foot usually contains one stressed syllable and at least one unstressed syllable. Meter gives poetry its rhythmic pattern.

Iambic: an unstressed syllable followed by a stressed syllable – English is by its nature an iambic language.

Trochee: a stressed syllable followed by one or more unstressed syllables. (There are five other meters.)

Pentameter: a line of poetry that has five feet. Here is an example of iambic pentameter: "Shall **I** com**pare** thee **to** a **sum**mer's **day**?" Here is an example to trochaic pentameter: "**Nev**er, **nev**er, **nev**er, **nev**er, **nev**er!"

Tetrameter: a line of poetry with four feet. Here is an example of iambic tetrameter: "Come **live** with **me** and **be** my **love**." Here is an example of trochaic tetrameter: "**Dou**ble, **dou**ble **toil** and **trou**ble; / **Fire** **burn**, and **cald**ron **bub**ble."

Onomatopoeia: when the pronunciation of a word actually mimics the sound of the object or action it describes (e.g., buzz, sizzling, yapping).

Rhyme scheme: the repeated pattern of rhyme that comes at the end of lines of poetry – full rhyme is when the stressed vowels and consonants sound identical (e.g., chain, brain) – half rhyme is when the stressed consonants match but the vowel sounds do not (e.g., long, swing).

Stanza / verse: four or more lines with the same length, meter, and rhyme scheme – like paragraphs in prose, stanzas are composed of connected thoughts separated from other stanzas by a space.

General Terms

Ambiguous, ambiguity: when a statement is unclear in meaning – ambiguity may be deliberate or accidental.

Analogy: a comparison which treats two things as identical in one or more specified ways.

Antagonist: a character or force opposing the protagonist.

Antithesis: the complete opposite of something.

Climax: the conflict to which the action has been building since the start of the play or story.

Colloquialism: the casual, informal mainly spoken language of ordinary people – often called "slang."

Connotation: the ideas, feelings and associations generated by a word or phrase.

Dark comedy: comedy which has a serious implication – comedy that deals with subjects not usually treated humorously (e.g., death).

Dialogue: a conversation between two or more people in direct speech.

Diction: the writer's choice of words in order to create a particular effect.

Equivocation: saying something which is capable of two interpretations with the intention of misrepresenting the truth.

Euphemism: a polite word for an ugly truth – for example, a person is said to be sleeping when they are actually dead.

Fallacy: a misconception resulting from incorrect reasoning.

First person: first person singular is "I" and plural is "we".

Foreshadowing: a statement or action which gives the reader a hint of what is likely to happen later in the narrative.

Genre: the type of literature into which a particular text falls (e.g. drama, poetry, novel).

Image, imagery: figurative language such as simile, metaphor, personification etc., or a description which conjures up a particularly vivid picture.

Imply, implication: when the text suggests to the reader a meaning which it does not actually state.

Infer, inference: the reader's act of going beyond what is stated in the text to draw conclusions.

Irony, ironic: a form of humor which undercuts the apparent meaning of a statement:

Conscious irony: irony used deliberately by a writer or character;

Unconscious irony: a statement or action which has significance for the reader of which the character is unaware;

Dramatic irony: when an action has an important significance that is obvious to the reader but not to one or more of the characters;

Tragic irony: when a character says (or does) something which will have a serious, even fatal, consequence for him/ her. The audience is aware of the error, but the character is not;

Verbal irony: the conscious use of particular words which are appropriate to what is being said.

Juxtaposition: literally putting two things side by side for purposes of comparison and/ or contrast.

Literal: the surface level of meaning that a statement has.

Melodramatic: action and/or dialogue that is inflated or extravagant – frequently used for comic effect.

Metaphor, metaphorical: the description of one thing by direct comparison with another (e.g. the coal-black night).

   Extended metaphor: a comparison which is developed at length.

Mood: the feelings and emotions contained in and/ or produced by a work of art (text, painting, music, etc.).

Motif: a frequently repeated idea, image or situation in a text.

Motivation: why a character acts as he/she does – in modern literature motivation is seen as psychological.

Narrator: the voice that the reader hears in the text – not to be confused with the author.

Oxymoron: the juxtaposition of two terms normally thought of as opposite (e.g. the silent scream).

Paradox, paradoxical: a statement or situation which appears self-contradictory and therefore absurd.

Pathos: is pity, or rather the ability of a text to make the audience or reader feel pity.

Perspective: point of view from which a story, or an incident within a story, is told.

Personified, personification: a simile or metaphor in which an inanimate object or abstract idea is described by comparison with a human.

Plot: a chain of events linked by cause and effect.

Protagonist: the character who initiates the action and is most likely to have the sympathy of the audience.

Realism: a text that describes the action in a way that appears to reflect life.

Sarcasm: stronger than irony – it involves a deliberate attack on a person or idea with the intention of mocking.

Setting: the environment in which the narrative (or part of the narrative) takes place.

Simile: a description of one thing by explicit comparison with another (e.g. my love is like a red, red rose).

Extended simile: a comparison which is developed at length.

Style: the way in which a writer chooses to express him/ herself. Style is a vital aspect of meaning since how something is expressed can crucially affect what is being written or spoken.

Symbol, symbolic, symbolism, symbolize: a physical object which comes to represent an abstract idea (e.g. the sun may symbolize life).

Themes: important concepts, beliefs and ideas explored and presented in a text.

Third person: third person singular is "he/ she/ it" and plural is "they" – authors often write novels in the third person.

Tone: literally the sound of a text – How words sound (either in the mouth of an actor or the head of a reader) can crucially affect meaning.

Selected Bibliography

Brown, Robert. *The Unity of "A Shropshire Lad"*. University of Richmond, Honors Thesis, Paper 651, *UR Scholarship Repository*. 1970. Web. 23 Nov. 2019.

Davenport, Basil and Tom Burns Haber. *Complete Poems A. E. Housman: Centennial Edition*. New York: Holt, Rinehart and Winston, 1959. Print.

Douglas-Fairhurst, Robert. "A. E. Housman: the laureate of repression." Lead Book Review, *The Spectator*. 2 Jul. 2016. Web. 29 Nov. 2019.

Firchow, Peter and Bernfried Nugel. *Reluctant Modernists: Aldous Huxley and Some Contemporaries*. Munster: Lit Verlag, 2002. Print.

Gow, A. S. F. *A. E. Housman A Sketch Together with a List of His Writings and Indexes to His Classical Papers*. Cambridge: Cambridge University Press, 1936. Print.

Graves, Richard. *A. E. Housman The Scholar-Poet*. New York: Charles Scribner's Sons, 1979. Print.

Haber, Tom. *A. E. Housman*. New York: Twayne Publishers, 1967. Print.

Hamilton, Robert. *A. E. Housman The Poet*. Exeter: Sydney Lee, 1953. Print.

Housman, A. E. *A Shropshire Lad*. 1919. Introduction by William Stanley Braithwaite. *Project Gutenberg EBook*. 2013. Web. 28 Nov. 2019.

Lea, Gordon. "Ironies and Dualities in *a Shropshire Lad*." Colby Quarterly, Volume 10, Issue 2, Article 4, p.71-79. Jun. 1973. *Digitalcommons*, Colby College. Web. 29 Nov. 2019.

Leggett, Bobby. *The Poetic Art of A. E. Housman Theory and Practice*. Lincoln: University of Nebraska, 1978. Print.

Leggett, Bobby. *Theme and Structure in Housman's "A Shropshire Lad"*. 1965. University of Florida, PhD Dissertation. *UFDCImages*. Web. 23 Nov. 2019.

Marlow, Norman. *A. E. Housman Scholar and Poet*. Minneapolis: University of Minnesota, 1958. Print.

Orwell, George. "Inside the Whale." 1940. *George Orwell: Inside the Whale*: orwell.ru/library/essays/ whale. Web. 25 Nov. 2019.

Ricks, Christopher. *A. E. Housman A Collection of Critical Essays*. Englewood Cliffs: Prentice-Hall, 1968. Print.

Skutsch, Otto. *A. E. Housman 1859-1936*. London: The Athlone Press, 1960. Print.

Spacey, Andrew. *Owlcation.* 10 Nov. 2017. Web. 21 Jun. 2019.

SparkNotes Editors. "SparkNote on Frost's Early Poems." SparkNotes.com. *SparkNotes LLC.* 2002. Web. 20 Jun. 2019.

About the Author

Ray Moore was born in Nottingham, England. He obtained his Master's Degree in Literature from Lancaster University and taught in secondary education for twenty-eight years before relocating to Florida with his wife. There he taught English and Information Technology in the International Baccalaureate Program. He is now a full-time writer and fitness fanatic and leads a reading group at a local library.

Website: http://www.raymooreauthor.com

Ray strives to make his texts the best that they can be. If you have any comments or question about this book *please* contact the author through his email: **villageswriter@gmail.com**

Also by Ray Moore:
Books are available from amazon.com and from barnesandnoble.com as paperbacks and some from online eBook retailers.

Fiction:

1066: Year of the Five Kings is a novel of the most consequential year in the history of England.

The Lyle Thorne Mysteries
If you enjoy detective short stories, you will love my series featuring policeman turned vicar Lyle Thorne (1860-1947)
Investigations of The Reverend Lyle Thorne (Volume One)
Further Investigations of The Reverend Lyle Thorne (Volume Two)
Early Investigations of Lyle Thorne (Volume Three)
Sanditon Investigations of The Rev. Lyle Thorne (Volume Four)
Final Investigations of The Rev. Lyle Thorne (Volume Five)
Lost Investigation of The Rev. Lyle Thorne (Volume Six)
Official Investigations of Lyle Thorne (Volume Seven)
Clerical Investigations of The Rev. Lyle Thorne (Volume Eight)

Non-fiction:
The **Critical Introduction series** is written for high school teachers and students and for college undergraduates. Each volume gives an in-depth analysis of a key text:
"The Stranger" by Albert Camus: A Critical Introduction (Revised Second Edition)
"The General Prologue" by Geoffrey Chaucer: A Critical Introduction
"Pride and Prejudice" by Jane Austen: A Critical Introduction

"The Great Gatsby" by F. Scott Fitzgerald: A Critical Introduction

The Text and Critical Introduction series <u>differs</u> from the Critical introduction series as these books contain the original text and in the case of the medieval texts an interlinear translation to aid the understanding of the text. The commentary allows the reader to develop a deeper understanding of the text and themes within the text.

"Sir Gawain and the Green Knight": Text and Critical Introduction*
"The General Prologue" by Geoffrey Chaucer: Text and Critical Introduction*
"Heart of Darkness" by Joseph Conrad: Text and Critical Introduction*
"Henry V" by William Shakespeare: Text and Critical Introduction*
"Oedipus Rex" by Sophocles: Text and Critical Introduction*
"A Room with a View" By E.M. Forster: Text and Critical Introduction*
"The Sign of Four" by Sir Arthur Conan Doyle Text and Critical Introduction
"The Wife of Bath's Prologue and Tale" by Geoffrey Chaucer: Text and Critical Introduction*
Jane Austen: The Complete Juvenilia: Text and Critical Introduction

Study Guides - listed alphabetically by author

Study Guides offer an in-depth look at aspects of a text. They generally include an introduction to the characters, genre, themes, setting, tone of a text. They also may include activities on helpful literary terms as well as graphic organizers to aid understanding of the plot and different perspectives of characters.

   * denotes also available as an eBook
"ME and EARL and the Dying GIRL" by Jesse Andrews: A Study Guide
Study Guide to "Alias Grace" by Margaret Atwood*
Study Guide to "The Handmaid's Tale" by Margaret Atwood*
"Pride and Prejudice" by Jane Austen: A Study Guide
"Moloka'i" by Alan Brennert: A Study Guide
"Wuthering Heights" by Emily Brontë: A Study Guide *
Study Guide on "Jane Eyre" by Charlotte Brontë*
"The Myth of Sisyphus" by Albert Camus: A Study Guide
"The Stranger" by Albert Camus: A Study Guide
"The Myth of Sisyphus" and "The Stranger" by Albert Camus: Two Study Guides *
Study Guide to "Death Comes to the Archbishop" by Willa Cather
"The Awakening" by Kate Chopin: A Study Guide
Study Guide to Seven Short Stories by Kate Chopin
Study Guide to "Ready Player One" by Ernest Cline
Study Guide to "Disgrace" by J. M. Coetzee
"The Meursault Investigation" by Kamel Daoud: A Study Guide
Study Guide on "Great Expectations" by Charles Dickens*
"The Sign of Four" by Sir Arthur Conan Doyle: A Study Guide *

A Shropshire Lad

Study Guide to "Manhattan Beach" by Jennifer Egan
"The Wasteland, Prufrock and Poems" by T.S. Eliot: A Study Guide
Study Guide on "Birdsong" by Sebastian Faulks*
"The Great Gatsby" by F. Scott Fitzgerald: A Study Guide
"A Room with a View" by E. M. Forster: A Study Guide
"Looking for Alaska" by John Green: A Study Guide
"Paper Towns" by John Green: A Study Guide
Study Guide to "Turtles All the Way Down" by John Green
Study Guide to "Florida" by Lauren Groff
Study Guide on "Catch-22" by Joseph Heller *
"Unbroken" by Laura Hillenbrand: A Study Guide
"The Kite Runner" by Khaled Hosseini: A Study Guide
"A Thousand Splendid Suns" by Khaled Hosseini: A Study Guide
"The Secret Life of Bees" by Sue Monk Kidd: A Study Guide
Study Guide on "The Invention of Wings" by Sue Monk Kidd
Study Guide to "Fear and Trembling" by Søren Kierkegaard
"Go Set a Watchman" by Harper Lee: A Study Guide
Study Guide to "Pachinko" by Min Jin Lee
"On the Road" by Jack Kerouac: A Study Guide
Study Guide on "Life of Pi" by Yann Martel*
Study Guide to "Death of a Salesman" by Arthur Miller
Study Guide to "The Bluest Eye" by Toni Morrison
Study Guide to "Reading Lolita in Tehran" by Azir Nafisi
Study Guide to "The Sympathizer" by Viet Thanh Nguyen
"Animal Farm" by George Orwell: A Study Guide
Study Guide on "Nineteen Eighty-Four" by George Orwell
Study Guide to "The Essex Serpent" by Sarah Perry
Study Guide to "Selected Poems" and Additional Poems by Sylvia Plath*
"An Inspector Calls" by J.B. Priestley: A Study Guide
Study Guide to "Cross Creek" by Marjorie Kinnan Rawlings
"Esperanza Rising" by Pam Munoz Ryan: A Study Guide
Study Guide to "The Catcher in the Rye" by J.D. Salinger
"Where'd You Go, Bernadette" by Maria Semple: A Study Guide
"Henry V" by William Shakespeare: A Study Guide
Study Guide on "Macbeth" by William Shakespeare *
"Othello" by William Shakespeare: A Study Guide *
Study Guide on "Antigone" by Sophocles*
"Oedipus Rex" by Sophocles: A Study Guide
"Cannery Row" by John Steinbeck: A Study Guide
"East of Eden" by John Steinbeck: A Study Guide
"The Grapes of Wrath" by John Steinbeck: A Study Guide
"Of Mice and Men" by John Steinbeck: A Study Guide*

209

"The Goldfinch" by Donna Tartt: A Study Guide
Study Guide to "The Hate U Give" by Angie Thomas
"Walden; or, Life in the Woods" by Henry David Thoreau: A Study Guide
Study Guide to "Cat's Cradle" by Kurt Vonnegut
"The Bridge of San Luis Rey" by Thornton Wilder: A Study Guide *
Study Guide on "The Book Thief" by Markus Zusak

Study Guides available *only* as e-books:

Study Guide on "Cross Creek" by Marjorie Kinnan Rawlings.
Study Guide on "Heart of Darkness" by Joseph Conrad.
Study Guide on "The Mill on the Floss" by George Eliot
Study Guide on "Lord of the Flies" by William Golding
Study Guide on "Nineteen Eighty-Four" by George Orwell
Study Guide on "Henry IV Part 2" by William Shakespeare
Study Guide on "Julius Caesar" by William Shakespeare
Study Guide on "The Pearl" by John Steinbeck
Study Guide on "Slaughterhouse-Five" by Kurt Vonnegut

New titles are added regularly.

Readers' Guides

Readers' Guides offer an introduction to important aspects of the text and questions for personal reflection and/or discussion. Guides are written for individual readers who wish to explore texts in depth and for members of Reading Circles who wish to make their discussions of texts more productive.

A Reader's Guide to Becoming by Michelle Obama
A Reader's Guide to Educated: A Memoir by Tara Westover

Teacher resources: Ray also publishes many more study guides and other resources for classroom use on the 'Teachers Pay Teachers' website: **http://www.teacherspayteachers.com/Store/Raymond-Moore**

Made in the USA
Columbia, SC
02 June 2021